"Francis X. Clooney, a pioneer in developing the method of 'comparative theology' through his own study of Hinduism, offers us an excellent and illustrative introduction to it by telling us the story of Hindu–Christian studies in India from an analytic perspective. The missionary approach of Christians and the defensive reaction of Hindus slowly evolve, helped by the modern study of religion, into the discovery of a common space where faith can meet faith without abandoning intellectual rigour or religious identity. Clooney carefully points to both the challenges and benefits of intelligent, attentive, theologically grounded exchange. The book is a 'must read' for anyone interested in comparative theology and in Hindu–Christian studies."

Michael Amaladoss, *Director of the Institute for Dialogue with Cultures and Religions, India*

"Francis X. Clooney, has carefully mapped Christian–Hindu interactions since their inception to now, demonstrating the longevity, sophistication, and complexity of those interactions, attending carefully to perspectives in each tradition. Highlighting forgotten instances wherein each took the other seriously, and couched in a sympathetic and nuanced Catholic theological perspective, The Future of Hindu–Christian Studies also addresses important issues arising in theology and religious studies today."

Jonathan Edelmann, *Assistant Professor of Religion, University of Florida, USA, and Affiliate Member, Center for the Study of Hindu Traditions*

"Judiciously and with characteristic lucidity, Francis X. Clooney analyzes various past and present attempts at Hindu–Christian Studies. His is one of the most interesting voices in the field of comparative theology today, challenging all scholars to revitalize their approach to dialogue and traverse new frontiers of academic and spiritual knowledge."

Anita C. Ray, *Faculty of Theology and Philosophy, and Comparative Theology, Interreligious Dialogue Network, Australian Catholic University, Australia*

"This insightful exploration of the history of intellectual engagement between Christians and Hindus also looks forward with clarity towards the prospects for continued dialogue. Clooney builds on his specialist scholarship to ask questions about the challenges facing comparative theology in the academy today, and offers insightful answers with sober optimism."

Chakravarthi Ram-Prasad, *Professor and Associate Dean for Research, Faculty of Arts and Social Sciences, Lancaster University, UK*

The Future of Hindu–Christian Studies

The field of Hindu–Christian studies revives theology as a particularly useful interreligious discipline. Though a sub-division of the broader Hindu–Christian dialogue, it is also a distinct field of study, proper to a smaller group of religious intellectuals. At its best it envisions a two-sided, mutual conversation, grounded in scholars' knowledge of their own tradition and of the other.

Based on the Westcott–Teape Lectures given in India and at the University of Cambridge, this book explores the possibilities and problems attendant upon the field of Hindu–Christian studies, the reasons for occasional flourishing and decline in such studies, and the fragile conditions under which the field can flourish in the 21st century. The chapters examine key instances of Christian–Hindu learning, highlighting the Jesuit engagement with Hinduism, the modern Hindu reception of Western thought, and certain advances in the study of religion that enhance intellectual cooperation.

This book is a significant contribution to a sophisticated understanding of Christianity and Hinduism in relation. It presents a robust defense of comparative theology and of Hindu–Christian studies as a necessarily theological discipline. It will be of wide interest in the fields of religious studies, theology, Christianity and Hindu studies.

Francis X. Clooney, SJ, is Parkman Professor of Divinity and Professor of Comparative Theology at Harvard Divinity School, Harvard University, USA. From 2010 to 2017, he was also the Director of the Center for the Study of World Religions. He is one of the foremost authorities in Hindu–Christian studies, and a leading proponent of comparative theology, a field of study which, though informed by philological scholarship and advances in the study of religion, respects the inner logic of faith traditions even while employing intellectual tools not defined by any one tradition.

Routledge Hindu Studies Series

Series Editor: Gavin Flood, Oxford Centre for Hindu Studies

A RECOGNISED INDEPENDENT CENTRE OF THE UNIVERSITY OF OXFORD

The *Routledge Hindu Studies Series*, in association with the Oxford Centre for Hindu Studies, intends the publication of constructive Hindu theological, philosophical and ethical projects aimed at bringing Hindu traditions into dialogue with contemporary trends in scholarship and contemporary society. The series invites original, high quality, research level work on religion, culture and society of Hindus living in India and abroad. Proposals for annotated translations of important primary sources and studies in the history of the Hindu religious traditions will also be considered.

Debating "Conversion" in Hinduism and Christianity
Ankur Barua

Non-violence in the Mahabharata
Siva's Summa on Rishidharma and the Gleaners of Kurukshetra
Alf Hiltebeitel

The other Ramayana Women
Regional Rejection and Response
Edited by John Brockington and Mary Brockington

The Integral Philosophy of Aurobindo
Hermeneutics and the Study of Religion
Brainerd Prince

Hindu Images and Their Worship with Special Reference to Vaisnavism
A philosophical-theological inquiry
Julius J. Lipner

River and Goddess Worship in India
Changing Perceptions and Manifestations of Sarasvati
R. U. S. Prasad

The Future of Hindu-Christian Studies
A Theological Inquiry
Francis X. Clooney

The Future of Hindu–Christian Studies

A Theological Inquiry

Francis X. Clooney, SJ

LONDON AND NEW YORK

First published 2017 by Routledge

2 Park Square, Milton Park, Abingdon, Oxfordshire OX14 4RN
52 Vanderbilt Avenue, New York, NY 10017

Routledge is an imprint of the Taylor & Francis Group, an informa business

First issued in paperback 2019

British Library Cataloguing in Publication Data
A catalogue record for this book is available from the British Library

Library of Congress Cataloging in Publication Data
Names: Clooney, Francis X. (Francis Xavier), 1950- author.
Title: The future of Hindu-Christian studies : a theological inquiry / Francis X. Clooney.
Description: New York : Routledge, 2017. | Series: Routledge Hindu studies series | Includes bibliographical references and index.
Identifiers: LCCN 2017013024 | ISBN 9781138696167 (hardback) | ISBN 9781315525259 (ebook)
Subjects: LCSH: Christianity and other religions--Hinduism. | Hinduism--Relations--Christianity.
Classification: LCC BR128.H5 C56 2017 | DDC 261.2/45--dc23
LC record available at https://lccn.loc.gov/2017013024

ISBN: 978-1-138-69616-7 (hbk)
ISBN: 978-0-367-88975-3 (pbk)

Typeset in Times New Roman
by Taylor & Francis Books

Contents

Foreword

Julius Lipner

The "Teape Lectures," as they are conveniently called, can be traced back as a series to 1955. Their broad remit has been to further understanding between the two religio-cultural streams generally referred to as "Hinduism" and "Christianity." Over the course of the last sixty years or so, many well-known scholars and thinkers, hitherto drawn from the subcontinent and the UK, have been Teape lecturers. Professor Clooney's distinguished contribution is the first from an American to be added to the list. As Chair of the Teape committee which oversees the choice of Teape Lecturer, I am privileged to be asked to write this foreword for what will undoubtedly become an indispensable contribution to our grasp of and engagement with the discipline of Hindu–Christian studies.

As Clooney notes, the history of Hindu–Christian studies has been a vexed one, not least in modern times, with numerous ups and downs in the study of the relationship between the two faiths. Yet for a number of reasons this has become an important discipline in the broad field of the study of religion. For one thing, it has acted as something of a marker of the development of study in the relationships between different faiths in general.

Clooney starts by "Framing the Question," where he affirms that the "field of Hindu–Christian studies envisions a two-sided, mutual conversation, grounded in scholars' knowledge of their own tradition and that of the other." This has not always been the case. He points out that hitherto the initiative has been from the Christian side, and begins his analysis by showing how early modern Christians from different faith-perspectives – here the focus is on the Jesuit missions to the East – took to their task with an intellectual gusto which, though well-meaning, ill served both their own and the target faith. As the book progresses, we are shown how the situation has been evening up with the passage of time. Hindu commentators on Christian and Western perspectives (often this distinction has been blurred) have increasingly adopted a more robust approach, pointing to colonial, linguistic, and financial imbalances in the past favoring the positions of their interlocutors. Clooney deftly and, in some depth, equitably reviews these arguments so as to put the reader in a better position to assess both the history and the present situation.

A controversial feature of Clooney's account is his insistence that "Hindu–Christian studies" must be essentially a theological enterprise, seeking a "third space" or common or neutral ground between the interlocutors which becomes explorative for both sides, and in which mistakes can be honestly made, risks taken, and genuinely new insights, views, and policies constructed.

As a theological inquiry – as an inquiry, that is, in which "faith seeks understanding" – "Hindu–Christian studies" then becomes an integral part of the study of religion, for it will be based on properly informed, even scholarly, points of view, but it will also be distinctive in so far as it is grounded on a stance of faith. Indeed, Clooney points out, all scholarship – and that of the study of religion is no exception – has inherent inquirer-biases which need to be acknowledged and suitably allowed for, and it has become something of a commonplace, he notes, and more acceptable for scholars in general (well, certainly in the study of religion), to function in accordance with this understanding.

All this has been carefully dissected and defended in this book, which makes of it all the more a valuable methodological exercise. Whether there will be consensus that "Hindu–Christian studies" must be a theological inquiry, whether in fact this will be judged to be too narrow a definition, remains to be seen. But even its contestation will no doubt produce fertile insights and take the discipline helpfully in new directions.

Clooney writes in a balanced and clear-sighted manner and discusses the views of a number of earlier and current thinkers from all sides of the argument, showing command of the field and the various positions analyzed. Our debt to him as inquirers in the study of religions and Hindu–Christian studies in particular, with regard to the acquisition of both scholarship and wisdom, will always remain a substantial one.

Acknowledgments

Every author is inevitably and gladly indebted to many colleagues and friends who help move her or his project along, from the earliest ideas to the final publication. A lecture series that becomes a book is all the more the product of the kindness of many near and far. I am first of all grateful to Julius Lipner, Chair of the Teape Trust, for extending the invitation to me in the first place, and for his patience as I slowly found identified January 2015 as the right time to give the Lectures in India. Both in the preparations, and in my May 2016 visit to Cambridge, where I gave a version of the Lectures, I am grateful as well to Jonathan Collis, Secretary of the Teape Trust, Chris Chivers and Paul Dominiak, co-Trustees of the Teape Trust, and Martin Seeley, former Trustee. During that visit, Professors Ankur Barua, Paul Dominiak, and Douglas Headley were also most gracious in extending a warm welcome, and Westcott House was the perfect place to spend a few days.

When I gave the Lectures in India in January 2015, I received a cordial welcome and great hospitality from friends and scholars in many places: in Chennai, at the Institute for the Dialogue of Cultures and Religions, Michael Amaladoss, SJ, and Vincent Sekhar, SJ, were my hosts, and at the University of Madras, Godabarisha Mishra (Philosophy) welcomed me; in Kolkata, Sunil Michael Caleb (Principal of Bishop's College) and the staff and students of the College were most welcoming and solicitous from the beginning to the end of my days there; in New Delhi, Valson Thampu was Principal of St. Stephen's College during my visit, and Fr. Monodeep Daniel, Head of the Brotherhood of the Ascended Christ and Dean of St. Stephen's College, was a gracious host. In each setting, numerous other faculty and students and good neighbors attended the Lectures and asked very good questions that have improved the final version of them included in this book.

These Lectures are also the fruit of more than four decades of experience in learning from Hinduism in its many forms, and from Hindu friends and colleagues – and occasional sparring partners – in Nepal and India, and here in the United States. Christian friends too, here and in South Asia and in communities such as the Society for Hindu–Christian Studies, have helped me to go deeper and appreciate the many benefits of a Christian learning from Hinduism, even while keeping me honest about the limits of my knowledge, the never-ending challenges of helping Christians to see the wisdom and truth of Hindu traditions, and the need, already, to place my hope in the next generations of scholars, Hindu and Christian, who will continue this vital collaboration and shared learning.

I am grateful also to friends at Harvard Divinity School, and particularly my staff at the Center for the Study of World Religions, who have encouraged my work and tolerated my many travels: Corey O'Brien, Associate Director, current staff members Dorie Goehring (who most efficiently and quickly put together the book's index). Ariella Ruth Goldberg, and Matthew Whitacre, and of course still-missed friends from the staff who have moved on to other positions: Charles Anderson, Alexis Gewertz Salomone, and Jane Anna Chapman.

Prologue

Framing the questions

The Westcott–Teape legacy

In January 2015, I gave the Westcott–Teape Memorial Lectures in New Delhi (St. Stephen's College), Kolkata (Bishop's College), and Chennai (Loyola College and the University of Madras). In May 2016, I gave a version of them again in the Divinity Faculty at the University of Cambridge, UK, where the Teape Trust is based.

The Lectures were instituted in honor of Brooke Foss Westcott (1825–1901), Cambridge Professor, Bishop of Durham, and among the founders of the Cambridge Mission to India, by his student, William Marshall Teape (1882–1944). This distinguished series dates back to 1955, and from the start has been dedicated to the cultivation of Hindu–Christian understanding.[1] In his *On Some Points in Religious Office of the Universities*, Westcott wrote of the necessarily limited grasp every culture can have on the truth of the Gospel, even simply because of the uncertainties of language:

> We forget that the value of words changes according to the conditions under which they are used; that the proportionate value of doctrines, if I may so speak, varies with the vicissitudes of the spiritual state; that our common manhood, which Christ redeemed, presents only in separate parts the whole richness of its capacities and wealth; that our essential Creed is a creed of facts which speak at once in the fullness of life to every form of life. The different characteristics of Greek and Latin and Teutonic Christianity are a commonplace with theological students; and can we doubt that India, the living epitome of the races, the revolutions, and the creeds of the East, is capable of adding some new element to the completer apprehension of the Faith?[2]

Accordingly, he thought it essential that Christianity respect and not obliterate other religious cultures. Reducing India to an exemplary instance of Western Christianity would in the end be a loss to Christendom, since

> We should lose the very lessons, which in the providence of God India has to teach us. We should lose the assurance of true victory which comes from the preservation and development of every power in the new citizens of the kingdom of Christ. We should lose the integrity, the vitality, the infinity of our faith, in the proud assertion of our own supremacy.[3]

Teape himself[4] was a notable personality. He wrote *The Secret Lore of India and the One Perfect Life for All, Being A Few Main Passages from the Upanisads.* In it he recounts his own search and his motivation for learning from Hinduism. At the start of the book, Teape recounts his early experience in learning a bit of Sanskrit, and his later determination, in a missionary spirit, to combat the enemies of the Gospel. His initial imagery was martial. He heard a sermon which described

> the Final Conflict for Christ which [the preacher] was confident was nigh, even the battle of Armageddon, when the sixth golden bowl of the wrath of God should be poured out and the war of the great day of God the Almighty should begin, foretold in the Revelation of St. John. Where should it be fought and with whom? Plainly in India and with Hinduism, Islam and Buddhism.[5]

To prepare himself for this "battle," Teape began to study Hinduism, which he explored with the help of the books by some of the great scholars of his era: Paul Deussen; Robert E. Hume, translator of the Upanisads; and writings on Veda and Vedanta from a quartet of well-known scholars – Shripad K. Belvalkar, Mahadev Govind Ranade, Arthur A. Macdonell, and Arthur B. Keith. This study seems first to have convinced him that Hinduism posed the greatest challenge to Christians, and made him simply a better-educated combatant.

At this point, fortunately, Westcott's vision seems to have guided Teape along a more irenic and fruitful path:

> "[Westcott] dreamed," as Susil Kumar Rudra writes, "of a new Alexandria on the banks of the Jumna." That is code for the fact that he sought to encourage inter-religious encounter and believed such encounter enriching to the life and faith of the individuals and communities involved. Just as the Jesus movement had passed through an epochal transformation, which laid the foundation for

> the making of Europe, in moving out from the Semitic, Palestinian cradle of its origins into the Graeco-Roman culture and society of the Mediterranean world, a culture and society represented for Westcott in its intellectual openness by the schools of Alexandria, so he believed that further historic transformations awaited its appropriation by Asia.[6]

Or as Teape himself sums it up,

> It was Westcott's dream in his Cambridge days … that a College of Indian students, trained, so he hoped, at his own university, Cambridge, should be founded to think out these problems so acutely felt by both Hindu and Christian. … "Is it," he asked; "too much to hope, that on the Indus or the Ganges should rise some new Alexandria?"[7]

Inspired then to a more irenic form of engagement, Teape fashioned his synthesis of Hinduism and Christianity, India and the West, with the help of Westcott's writings. Speaking of himself in the third person, Teape notes how Westcott taught him to see that "the Upanishad fathers are like prospectors who have caught sight, in outline and with not a little mist obscuring their view, what has been revealed in such fullness and clearness to the Christian." This judgment enabled, rather than thwarted, Teape's more positive next step: "Revelation has a history. A waiting of the world had to be until the Fuller Light should break in. So here is not strife but a recognition of Fellow-seekers after Truth." In this context, Teape adds, the battle therefore is not against one or another religion, but rather against those forms of darkness and wickedness "which beset and hinder the understanding and the endeavors of all men in their pursuit of a life of devotion to the Highest."[8] It is important here to estimate this heritage soberly, without naively accepting it all or abruptly dismissing it all. Westcott and Teape were Christian apologists, driven by faith to the study of Hinduism. Had they not been interested in Christ's presence everywhere in the world, they would not have formed an inclusive Christian vision and would not have found India so interesting a place and prospect.

In any case, the synthesis of Westcott's and Teape's views underlay what came to be the Westcott–Teape Lectures: "The advancement of education by the provision of lectures on the relationship between Christian and Hindu thought and subject thereto the study of Christian and Hindu religious thought and the promotion of Christian–Hindu relations." Beginning with Charles E. Raven's lecture in 1955,[9] numerous distinguished scholars have traveled from India to the UK, and the UK to India, to give the Lectures.[10] I am honored that in 2015 I joined the list, as the first American to give the Lectures.

The very idea of Hindu–Christian studies

Hindu–Christian studies may be seen as a sub-division of the broader Hindu–Christian dialogue. But it is also necessary to see this as a distinct field of study, proper to a smaller group of religious intellectuals. Accordingly, at the core of these lectures is my own view of Hindu–Christian studies as a valuable, even if ever imperfect, field of study, a kind of interreligious theology. By this I mean, to draw on an old Christian formulation, the disposition and practice of *faith seeking understanding*. It is thus to be distinguished from a faith enclosed upon itself or immune to the benefits and challenges of inquiry, but also from any mode of reasoning that merely distances itself from faith, religious community, and religious practice. This theological rendering of Hindu–Christian studies is workable, I have found, even if it is narrower than some will prefer. It suggests that *study* is a theological enterprise comprised of intellectual and spiritual scholarship, the learning of individuals conscious of and responsible to ancient and living communities of readers and of believers. The form of "*study*" I have in mind when I talk about Hindu–Christian studies is therefore a deep learning grounded in both heart and mind, and performed by Christians learning Hinduism, ideally alongside Hindus learning Christianity. In accord with the wisdom of both traditions, this study of the Other requires the cultivation *together* of intellectual and spiritual components of learning, in a holistic appropriation characteristic of integral intellectual religious traditions. It will be open to the spiritual and transformative dimensions of the texts that are studied. In such study, the persons of the other tradition are respected as persons, to whom one is intellectually and ethically responsible; the doctrines of the other tradition are respected as possessed of practical as well as theoretical implications worthy of regard, as peers to the philosophical and theological reflection of one's home tradition, and as probably transformative and true. Such study may be enacted in the work of the individual scholar on her or his own, or in dialogue and active collaboration, in academic or other intellectually marked situations, among Hindu and Christian intellectuals. The field of Hindu–Christian studies envisions a two-sided, mutual conversation, grounded in scholars' knowledge of their own tradition and of the other tradition. If so, we need to shift our gaze from area studies and history to the work of religious intellectuals; this is a revival of theology as a particularly useful interreligious discipline. In a way, a community forms that is reducible to neither tradition.

I recognize that Hindu–Christian studies must in some way be a dialogical discipline, a great and ongoing conversation, but in the short run it is viable as a solitary study that relies on personal reflection, even if only later on does it open up into conversation through teaching, lecturing, and writing.[11] In the three lectures that are the core of this little book, we will often enough see how religious energies and spiritual certainties drive both Christian and Hindu interest in the other, making a more comprehensive vision possible, such as may welcome the other or, sadly, attempt to consume and dominate it. Generative energy and the imperfection of religious ambition often go together. But we cannot afford to be purists who demand only total neutrality or a benign and relativistic flattening of all differences as the basis for interreligious learning. If we ignore or explain away the passions and conviction of faith, we will have left a proper Hindu–Christian study behind from the start. This is not to say that today we are therefore licensed to impugn or condescend to religions other than our own; ours is an age of reciprocal learning, where faith makes deeper exchange possible; but we cannot, for the sake of openness, merely disown narratives and dispositions of faith more narrow or hegemonic than our own.

The problem of Hindu–Christian studies: is there such a thing?

Of course, not everyone agrees that Hindu–Christian studies is possible or desirable. A key version of the problem was stated memorably in 1996 by Fred Clothey, a long-time friend to the field who nevertheless challenged its would-be practitioners:

> There are times I think the term Hindu–Christian "studies" or even Hindu–Christian "dialogue" is a misnomer and a fantasy. This is so for several reasons. 1. For one thing, there is a long history in which such "study" or conversation has been a monologue, a one-way street or an interpretation by imposition. There has been too much shouting at each other from caves and not enough honesty, negotiation, and mutual respect of personhood on the boundaries between where peoples live. 2. For another, such engagements are not and never again can be merely one on one discourses between persons with single identities. We are each increasingly persons with multiple identities, in the process of

> becoming different persons even as we "dialogue." None of us truly represents whatever "authentic" Christianity or Hinduism is supposed to be. 3. Nor can any of us speak, listen, or study in isolation from the dynamics of global processes where multiple forces and multiple religions impinge on one's self-representations. 4. Not only that: I have been increasingly pessimistic that whatever some of us as individuals may do or think, a vast majority of our coreligionists remain blissfully unaware of the need for inter-religious understanding or the desirability of rethinking fundamental metaphors in light of such conversations.[12]

Monologue; individualistic; subsumed within larger social and political forces; elitist: all of these dangers are fairly noted by Clothey, but seen from another angle, they are simply the darker and dangerous side of what are also virtues: self-expression in hopes of a hearing and response; individual acts that are influenced by but also influential upon the greater movements in society and culture; expert thought and action responsible to and at the service of the greater communities to which individuals belong, noting but resisting the mere politicization of religious exchanges.

Still, troubles abound. Even the idea of speaking and writing from a tradition is more difficult than in the past. Many younger people, including emerging scholars, fall into the category of "spiritual but not religious" or, perhaps more aptly for many, "meaningfully spiritual, nominally religious." They often do not think of themselves as belonging to a set tradition, and as a result, the very idea of stable bounds between the Hindu and Christian, such as can be confirmed and then crossed over intentionally, is called into question. If no one can identify as Hindu or Christian, either the field becomes impossible, or it will have to find a new way to flourish beyond the ordinary models we are accustomed to.

Addressing similar anxieties from another angle, Jan Peter Schouten suggests that the kind of mutual study ambitioned here may be on the wane, even as the resources for such study multiply. He reports a decline in Hindu interest in Christ and Christianity in recent decades. There is a long history of interaction, to be sure,

> but it is remarkable that in the past quarter of a century the voice of Hindus in the dialogue has grown silent. Both in religious schools and in more socially oriented movements, attention for the person of Jesus Christ is fading. And there is hardly any response when the ecclesiastical world in India calls on Hindus to continue

> the dialogue. Almost all of the Indian Christians who have applied themselves to the discussion with Hindus are disappointed by the lack of response.

He then quotes Jesuit Ignatius Puthiadam, who admits, seemingly despondent, that "Dialogue is mostly a Christian thing."[13] A host of dysfunctions infect the field: monologues, rather than serious mutual learning; the rejection of the very idea of anyone speaking for Hinduism or Christianity as wholes; the myriad political, economic, forces, quite aside from theology, that militate against shared and mutually transformative study; and, once more, the inevitable elitism of that small group which chooses to pursue these matters.

But we need not be merely negative, and we cannot afford to be. We can learn from one another, by a learning that is a kind of wisdom and a kind of participation, which does not cease to be scholarly as well. That we can and do learn, a benefit from learning, makes Hindu–Christian studies possible and valuable. But we need to find ways to narrow down the field to some better ways of study, as I shall attempt in the lectures that follow. Hence my insistence that Hindu–Christian studies is a kind of theology: it cannot simply be the sum total of all that is said by everyone who studies Hinduism and studies Christianity, or even the sum total of any and all theological and philosophical, sociological and historical studies that somehow pertain to Hinduism and Christianity. If the constructive nature of this learning – from and for Hindu and Christian communities that are open to learning from one another – is lost sight of, then it swiftly devolves into a kind of historical study about Christian–Hindu relations, a worthy but insufficient field. If its intellectual edge is too much blunted, it becomes identical with interreligious dialogue as the modest exchange that is necessary for civility and life together.

Admission of a mixed history

Hindu–Christian studies is blessed and burdened with a relatively long ancestry, and is today still vexed by the scars of old wounds never quite healed: missionary and colonialist appropriations of religions of India in a distortive fashion; the widely recognized problematic construction of a "Hinduism" then found to counter a (sometimes similarly simplified and ahistorical) Christianity; Hindus who view "theology" skeptically and with suspicion; more recent shifts in religious studies away from constructive theological work; and the rise of political forces that reject the very idea of encounter and mutual learning. Hindu–Christian studies may shift from a field in the humanities, enlivened by faith, to a more stable and safer realm of academic study that may more readily be characterized as simply historical retrieval or simply sociological. But the decline in missionary fervor is a mixed blessing if it also marks a decline in positive and constructive interest in the other at all.

We are, in addition, still faced with the difficult history of lack of knowledge, inadequate and asymmetrical access to knowledge, and too often, by way of ignorance, a deterioration into polemic, both the merely anti-intellectual kind, yet also a more sophisticated post-colonialist and post-orientalist critique of the other, even of the other's interest in one's own. At the same, time, the rise of a more extreme Hindu right aggravates the situation and makes mutually informative and transformative study – such as Hindu–Christian studies should be – harder to justify.

Hope for the future must remain mindful of the past in a way that neither romanticizes nor demonizes it. We ought not disown that past, not because nothing has changed, but because we can learn from the dynamics of past failures and successes how much to expect and how much to tolerate of our prejudices and ambiguities. Plausible, even if skewed and flawed, Hindu–Christian exchanges have occurred many times over the centuries, and religious intellectuals in each tradition have successfully learned from the other, and by this learning changed how Hindus and Christians think of their own traditions. The fact is important: Hindu–Christian studies have occurred, and therefore they can occur again. But this will always be a fragile field that can flourish only in special circumstances, where groundedness in tradition co-exists with intellectual and spiritual openness, and where personal study opens into and welcomes a communal Hindu–Christian conversation among religious intellectuals who believe that something intellectual and religious is to be gained by actual study and actual learning. The field is viable, even if always imperfectly, when the right combination of essential academic, communal, and spiritual dispositions converge. When the conditions are lacking, the potential field of study reduces to polemics uninformed by knowledge of the other, or to a non-theological academic study that flattens the multi-dimensional exchanges involved, thus leading to a simple neglect of Hindu–Christian studies altogether.[14]

My three lectures were meant to highlight some of the key issues, to deepen our sense of the past of this field, and, in the end, to call attention to choices to be made if the field is to flourish now. My lectures are a small contribution to the great issues at stake, and are not meant to be comprehensive, nor even entirely novel. I readily admit indebtedness to the work of many scholars, which is certainly not to be replaced by these lectures. Raymond Schwab's *The Oriental Renaissance: Europe's Rediscovery of India and the East, 1680–1880* (1984 tr.), Wilhelm Halbfass's *India and Europe: An Essay in Understanding* (1988 tr.), Ronald Inden's *Imagining India* (1990), and S. N. Balagangadhara's *"The Heathen in His Blindness...": Asia, the West, and the Dynamic of Religion* (1994). There are also more recent and fine-tuned works such as *German Orientalism in the Age of Empire: Religion, Race, and Scholarship* (2009) by Suzanne L. Marchand, *The Birth of Orientalism* (2010) by Urs App, and *Catholic Orientalism: Portuguese Empire, Indian Knowledge (16th–18th Centuries)* (2015) by Angela Barreto Xavier and Ines G. Županov. Notable too is Bob Robinson's *Christians Meeting Hindus: An Analysis and Theological Critique of the Hindu–Christian Encounter in India* (2004), a book that focuses specifically on the history and nature of religious and theological encounters, and locates them in the context of the wider relations of Hindus and Christians. Hugh Nicholson's *Comparative Theology and the Problem of Religious Rivalry* (2011) is insightful on the return of comparative theology, and, in that context, offers a valuable re-reading of Rudolph Otto's *Mysticism East and West* (1932), in order to detect how Otto was ultimately (mis)using Sankara in a defense of Eckhart and the Christian tradition. As will be clear in Lecture Three, we also cannot afford to ignore critical voices in the wider Hindu community, including recent figures such as Sita Ram Goel, Ram Swarup, and Rajiv Malhotra.

Such works help us to step back from the immediate, engaged Hindu study of the Christian and Christian study of the Hindu, and observe the phenomenon: both the Christian and Hindu scholars, and related philosophical and secular scholars, have worked, as we do today, within the very much broader panorama of how the West and India have engaged one another. As Halbfass's book shows most famously, these mutual traditions of study have overlapping, even if distinctive, dynamics. How we think of Hindu–Christian studies today – and how someone like me lectures on the topic – needs to be read in light of the much longer, linked and entangled versions of mutual study. Both the positive insights and the events of intellectual violence and the inevitable dilemmas all have long histories that we need to be aware of today.

The quest for a shared space for Hindu–Christian studies

What is needed, then, is a conducive space that is not the sole property of either tradition, and is not deracinated and inimical to both. For the purposes of this book we hold in our vision a "third space" in which Hindu and Christian intellectuals can meet, learn from one another fruitfully and in a way that demeans neither tradition, and facilitate a learning possible only in that shared space. Though I will generally use the term in a non-technical sense, we might recall how Homi Bhabha has described this uncertain space where two or more individuals/cultures interact. It "challenges our sense of the historical identity of culture as a homogenizing, unifying force, authenticated by the originary Past, kept alive in the national tradition of the People."[15] This unsettled area of discourse "displaces the narrative of the Western nation … written in homogeneous, serial time."[16] As a result, "hierarchical claims to some innate originality or 'purity' of cultures are untenable."[17] A third space, "though unrepresentable in itself," by way of supplement and alternative "constitutes the discursive conditions of enunciation that ensure that the meaning and symbols of culture have no primordial unity or fixity; that even the same signs can be appropriated, translated, rehistoricized, and read anew."[18]

It is useful to note two theological readings of "third space." First, in *The Hybrid Church in the City* (2007), Christopher Baker surveys a wider set of views on third space, including those of Edward Soja. In a pertinent chapter, "Toward a Theology of the Third Space," Baker highlights six features of our new hybrid, third space situation, the first three of which are applicable as we think about Hindu–Christian studies. First, there is the "theology of blurred encounters," in which the limits of language, the partial impenetrability of the other, and the impossibility of entirely stable understandings of self and other are key features. While stability in language and reliability in relationship is desirable, there are limits to the possibility of achieving such; one must both welcome the other, and learn to live with the uncertainties such hospitality brings. Second, hospitality will always be a risk, since even healthy relationships between groups will always unsettle both. As Baker puts it, there are the risk of wanting to consume the other, make it simply part of one's own self, and the risk of being eaten, disempowered by the arrival of the other, one's own identity giving way before the other. Third, the third space situation of our era entails a catholicity such as Robert Schreiter has described with respect to the Roman Catholic tradition: "deterritorialization," with concomitant compressions of time and space, and the new prominence of sheer difference, rather than territorial difference, as the key challenge; "multiple belonging," how, "by the compression of time, the world of cyberspace and the movement of peoples, … people are now participating in different realities at the same time," by a cultural dynamic that also entails fragmentation of the safe boundaries of home traditions.[19] In the new ordinary situation, in which purity of self and culture and religion is unattainable, the efforts to define self over against the other become increasingly difficult, if not impossible. Such factors remind us that the quest for a third space appropriate to the Hindu–Christian encounter, distanced from religious aggression, cultural contempt, and colonial power, will continue to be difficult, not merely because of how some religious people continue to act, but also because the achieved spaces for encounter will almost inevitably be unstable, unsettling, and never spaces in which set identities are merely displayed, honored, and safely stored away. If Hindu–Christian studies needs a space, it will always be a risky third space that never ceases to need the care and caution of those who would dwell there together. But this is not impossible, provided that, once again, we maintain vigilance in the face of tendencies to make this space a-religious or inimical to religion.

Ulrich Winkler likewise echoes Homi Bhabha's claims regarding the impossibility of "pure cultures," but then identifies hybridity as a key presupposition for comparative theological learning:

> The theoretical recognition of the split-space of enunciation may open the way to conceptualizing an international culture, based not on the exoticism or multiculturalism of the diversity of cultures but on the inscription and articulation of culture's hybridity. … By exploring this hybridity, this "Third Space," we may elude the politics of polarity and emerge as the others of ourselves.

While a focus on multiculturalism makes the phenomenon itself the center of attention, Ulrich adds, "the hybridity of the 'third space' inscribes discourses of difference into identity, not just of plurality."[20] In this new situation, "comparative theology could take on a significant meaning through responsibly and competently leading these discourses," such that existing discourses are not merely preserved or abruptly rejected, but rather "implemented and deepened." Comparative theology's experimental nature eschews generalizations and second-order claims, and by refusing to seize upon firm theories, it ensures that "no new imperiums of third spaces will be established as places of refuge beyond the traditions according to antiquated theories of space established."[21] Consequently, in a Hindu–Christian studies that maintains its theological edge without settling for dogmatism, we find a non-reductively defined "third space" where the communities and individuals in encounter do not lose their home identities, nor reify one through the defeat of the other. But if this third space is to retain its value, it will require the ongoing cooperative work of some Hindu and Christian intellectuals who are interested in the intellectual and spiritual values and committed to an ongoing and never-finished practice of interreligious learning that is intellectual and academic, spiritual and religious.

Writing as a Catholic Christian scholar of Hinduism

My own understanding of theology, and the kind of thinking it implies, arises from a Roman Catholic stance, mainstream in some ways, uniquely indebted to Hindu learning in other ways; the Catholic perspective enables this project, but burdens it with a certain history of misunderstandings too. Of course, to have read the history of Hindu–Christian studies through the lens of Protestant India would also have made a difference, and I by no means wish to imply that those alternatives are unimportant; they have simply not been the topic of my lectures.

For more than four decades I have studied Hinduism as a Catholic Christian; I have learned enormously and for the better. I have many Hindu friends, some of whom I have known since I first lived in Kathmandu in the mid-1970s. Mutual learning has occurred in many ways over the years. I am hopeful too because I believe that Hinduism and Christianity are consonant traditions which can endlessly enrich one another. This claim of stability has grounding in each of the traditions. In order that the reader know where I am coming from, I wish to recollect here, in the following six paragraphs, a statement I made at a May 2015 Hindu–Christian dialogue meeting at the Durga Temple, Virginia, on the harmony of Hindu and Christian traditions:

> For millennia, Hindus and Christians have been in relationship, first in India and now across the world. This is a living relationship, with the ups and downs, dark and light moments, of human experience, and it continues to take new forms even today. This ongoing communication makes us aware that Hindus and Christians have much to be thankful for, need reconciliation, and share many opportunities for future collaboration. Today, we can and should be spiritual friends and collaborators, friends in the work of spiritual renewal. Catholics everywhere are eager for a positive relationship, for the Church is also catholic, a universal community, even finding its place, now on respectful terms, in every culture old and new. It makes no sense for Catholic Christians to imagine that Hindu traditions are somehow outside or apart from the mystery and love of God manifest in Jesus Christ. Most deeply, the

Catholic vision of the world implies recognizing with gratitude that God works deeply and continually in the lives, words and actions, faith and practice, of devout Hindus of every tradition.

A fruitful Hindu–Catholic relationship is not merely a matter of necessity or convenience, but a truly spiritual opportunity with firm foundations. God is one; we are all the children of God; God wills the salvation and well-being of all; God is a mystery, ever greater than our efforts at exact definitions and boundaries. Fifty years ago, Vatican II opened up a new era in how Catholics and Hindus might relate. Nostra Aetate ("In Our Age") briefly described the Hindu paths of action, wisdom, and love, and then stated that the Church "rejects nothing that is true and holy" in Hinduism and other religions. It adds, "Indeed, she regards with sincere reverence those ways of conduct and of life, those precepts and teachings which, though differing in many aspects from the ones she holds and sets forth, nonetheless often reflect a ray of that Truth which enlightens all men." How can this be? It is because Jesus is "the way, the truth, and the life." (John 14:6); from a Catholic perspective, Jesus is radiant and alive in whatever paths lead to God, whatever is true, whatever is alive.

Hindu learning and wisdom invite Catholics to think anew about matters of theological importance: the nature of divine and how the divine is revealed to us; the importance of God's entrance into the world and of sacramental realities; the importance of seeing and affirming God as a person; the possibilities and limits of images and words about the divine reality; the riches and limits of ritual practice; who we ourselves are, as embodied beings subject to birth and death; the delicate balance between affirming the true, the good, and the beautiful, and respecting very diverse paths; the promise of liberation for all beings, over time. Learning all this is a blessed opportunity for Catholics, and so new ideas and insights find their way into our Catholic minds and hearts.

Since Vatican II, lived experience, study, shared learning, and work together on issues of justice have shown the urgency and fruitfulness of collaboration among Hindus and Catholics in India and globally. Innumerable small connections, so local as hardly to be noticed by media too often focused on bad news, make the relationship real. Leaders, monks, and scholars too have a role, but the firmest grounding of the Hindu–Christian relationship is found in ordinary life, in the cities and towns where we are neighbors to one another.

Hindus and Catholics share a sense of the wholeness of the natural and human worlds, a reverence for life in all forms, a

> recognition of deep spiritual truths; energized by our faiths, we can work together for the benefit of the world sorely in need of such values. In a world troubled by violence, environmental degradation, materialism, and widening gaps between rich and poor, Hindu–Catholic cooperation is all the more necessary.
>
> In spiritual practice too Hindus and Catholics have much in common, and much to learn from one another. We value quiet, mystical paths of the ascent of God. We celebrate the divine presence in nature. We recognize the special ways in which God is makes certain places holy. We build beautiful temples and churches, filled with sacraments and symbols, rites and music, that raise our minds and hearts to God. We can teach one another how better to be reverent, to worship, to find God in all things. It is good then that we meet and share our spiritual lives and journeys, now more than ever.[22]

I have quoted myself at length in order to be candid about my own starting points, stated in public at an interreligious event between the lectures (January 2015) and this book (completed in the winter of 2016–17). I speak from experience. I am a Catholic priest, a Jesuit, and for more than forty years I have studied, learned from, been transformed by my study of Hindu traditions. My work is for the most part the work of a scholar; and yet it has been intensely personal, words and ideas circumscribed in the entirety of a way of life. All of this is background which disposes me to find Hindu–Christian studies possible, actual, and important. I cannot say what Bishop Westcott or Dr. Teape might think of the pages to follow, but I do believe they would find familiar the instinct for intellectual and spiritual exchange that underlie my proposals.

Outline of the book

Lecture One follows a single trajectory of Christian learning about and from Hinduism: the Catholic Jesuit study of Hinduism. I chose this topic for my first lecture because it has long been familiar to me, and because of the instructive nature of this Jesuit erudition. It played out over four centuries, was in many ways pioneering, but, in the end, was pushed to the side by other concerns, urgent social needs, and preferences for direct action instead of longer-term learning. Over and again, we see the intense engagement of Jesuit intellectuals in the study of Hinduism, and their efforts pioneered the reception of Hinduism in Europe. The motivations for that study changed over time, but certain habits persisted, such as the polemical edge to some of the Jesuit scholarship, and its stubborn distance from internal Hindu understanding of the same ideas, texts, and practices. Accordingly, I have drawn comparisons and contrasts among figures such as Roberto de Nobili, Jean Venance Bouchet, Gaston-Laurent Coeurdoux, Brahmabandhab Upadhyay (who, though not a Jesuit, greatly influenced several generations of Jesuits), William Wallace, Pierre Johanns, Richard de Smet, Ignatius Hirudayam, and still more recent Jesuits. By doing so, I have hoped to highlight the elusive and fragile harmony – not to be idealized and never certain – that is required for Hindu–Christian study to proceed. On the one hand, serious study, motivated by intellectual and spiritual concerns, is necessary, and must be undertaken by individual, sometimes solitary scholars; on the other, such study must be pursued in ways and for reasons intelligible to the home community and also to the community that is studied. If this learning is marginal to the former or unwelcome to the latter, its delicate balance and subtle contribution will be sure to fail. It is not that the Jesuit Indologists failed, but that the work of making this scholarship relevant has to be renewed again and again.

Lecture Two pays close attention to the ways in which select Hindu intellectuals have received, studied, and responded to Western and Christian thought, and sought to find a common ground, a space in which the traditions might be thought together fairly and productively. I notice just several important Hindu intellectuals (writing in English) who may be counted as exemplars of the Hindu manner of engagement, including Brajendranath Seal, Algondavilli Govindacharya, Kotta Satchidananda Murty, Bimal Krishna Matilal, Sarvepalli Radhakrishnan, Daya Krishna, Arvind Sharma, and Anantanand Rambachan. Even if eschewing theological terms and perhaps not conceiving of their work as Hindu–Christian studies, they show us how Hindus have engaged the West with intellectual credibility and a clear insistence on the wider spiritual space in which intellectual exchange is to occur. Here too there is a certain fragility to the encounters. Some of this solid intellectual work has not gained due attention on the global scene and among Christian intellectuals, has overlooked natural allies in the Christian theological traditions, and at times has claimed perennial spiritual continuities that seemed substitutes for harder intellectual work, including studying Western and Christian traditions in depth, in original languages, etc. The weight of such work has tended toward a philosophy that keeps its distance from theology and occasionally gives the impression of also keeping spirituality at bay. The syntheses crafted by these Hindu intellectuals, if seen as too academic and too individual, may also be sidelined even in their own Hindu traditions, first distanced from popular sentiment and later drowned out by political voices impatient with the slow work of scholarship.

Lecture Three shifts the focus to the contemporary academic scene. Here I argue that a new frame, such as is provided in the academic study of religions has the potential to free up the possibilities we have discovered in the history of the Christian study of Hinduism and of the Hindu study of Christianity, find a way around the impasses of intellectual misrecognition and spiritual cannibalism, in order to perform the holistic religious intellectual work that rebalances the intellectual and the spiritual in a holistic communal synthesis. Even if the major site of Hindu–Christian exchange is likely to remain Indian, and even if Indian Hindus and Christians need not be advised yet again to learn from the West, nevertheless the grounding and motivation for Hindu–Christian studies in the future will pass through the modern academic milieu, chastened and refocused by critical work in the study of religions. Here too, caution is required, since there are uncertainties deeply imbedded in the academic study of religion, regarding whether it is one of the humanities, or a historical discipline, or a social science; whether it is inescapably Christian, or inimical to the theological and communal instincts of Christianity as well as those of Hinduism; and whether its intellectual work can be also a spiritual work that can revitalize Hindu–Christian studies. On the whole, I suggest, certain versions of the contemporary study of religion usefully reset the program and possibilities for the Christian study of Hinduism and the Hindu study of Christianity, while Hindu–Christian studies calls to the fore a true and fruitful strand within the wider study of religions.

Though selective and not comprehensive, the three lectures map the possibilities and problems facing Hindu–Christian studies. Or to put it very simply: the first lecture reflects on the "Christian," the second on the "Hindu," and third on the "studies." Taken together, they build the case that Hindus and Christians on their own, and then together, can cooperate in clearing the way a richly reciprocal intellectual and spiritual learning, the substance of Hindu–Christian studies.

My Epilogue, written for this book, goes beyond the lectures, elaborating on this richer and more fruitful Hindu–Christian learning by stressing its theological foundations. That is to say, Hindu–Christian studies is most naturally a theological project, albeit one that is inclusive of its important philological and historical, sociological and philosophical components. It requires intellectuals on both sides to resist historical and political reductionism, and instead allow the truths and values of traditions to shape a place and practice for Hindu–Christian learning. This theological grounding supports and frames the Hindu study of the Christian and the Christian study of the Hindu. It enables a mutual recognition by Hindu intellectuals and Christian intellectuals of their parallel studies and the cultivation of a mutual expectation and dependence, without which the intellectual work reduces again to an objectification of the other, the spiritual to a disrespectful consumption of the other, and the promise inherent in the hyphen – Hindu–Christian – to a lesser pairing of two monologues. The field can flourish with a just use of the names "Hindu" and "Christian" (which make most sense theologically) only if there is in place a shared, or potentially shareable, view of reality, such that intellectual exchange can occur, without its reduction to history or politics or sociology. I illustrate these claims by reference to my own work, and by holding up for consideration some excellent examples, recent books by notable scholars in the field.

I must make one more point here: all that follows, excepting the Epilogue, simply fills out and tidies up the three lectures, and remains thus limited in scope to what might be accomplished in that form. I have admitted already that the lectures keep touching on issues others have explored in more depth, while, I am sure, hardly mentioning issues that one or another reader might find important. They are essays, experiments, soundings into deeper and wider issues that, if successful, may shed light on the broader context wherein each lecture, as an example, has its place. My hope is that their overall effect is to be suggestive of the prospects and problems inherent in Hindu–Christian studies, and to make the case for one solution to the multi-dimensional problem, a mode of study that is essentially faith-grounded and community-grounded, and yet always deeply dialogical as well. I do not imagine that I am finishing off a discussion of these issues, but do hope to re-focus our conversation.

I am not a historian, nor expert on all the matters arising in these lectures. And yet, as mentioned, I write from long experience, and I believe that my theological perspective, guided by a hermeneutic of sympathy, promises a potentially distinctive contribution. I have thought about these matters for many years indeed, from the time of my first visits to Nepal and India in 1973–1975, and during subsequent studies, in teaching at Boston College and Harvard University, and by way of lectures at home and abroad, and in writing books, articles, and blogs over the decades. I have been a member of the Society for Hindu–Christian Studies since its founding nearly three decades ago, and am honored to have served as its first president. And so it is that the view of the past, present, and future of Hindu–Christian studies that emerges here represents my personal effort to consider in a coherent way a large and rich tradition of study, its ailments and a remedy for them. The results will be not entirely novel, but my hope is that readers will find valuable a view of Hindu–Christian studies observed, practiced, and tested over many years of experience.

Notes

1 An online history (http://ase.tufts.edu/chemistry/kumar/ssc/html/sschis.html) of St. Stephen's summarizes the story of the Lectures in this way: "The Rt. Revd. Brooke Foss Westcott, D. D., Bishop of Durham, and Regius Professor of Divinity, Cambridge was the first Chairman of the Cambridge Mission. To commemorate Bishop Westcott, the Westcott Memorial lectures, sponsored by the Teape Foundation, were started in 1955. The Revd. William Marshall Teape was a lover of India and a life-long disciple of the Revd. Westcott. Canon Charles E. Raven, the then Professor of Divinity at Cambridge, was the first Westcott Lecturer who delivered a series of eight talks on religion, science and technology in November 1955."

2 1873: 32–33.

3 Ibid., 33–34.

4 On Teape, see Jarvis 1990.

5 Teape 1932: ix.

6 As cited by Dan O'Connor 1994: x.

7 Teape 1932: 338–339.

8 Ibid.: xiii.

9 Raven's lecture was, "Hinduism and Christianity: A Neglected Crisis," delivered in 1955. The lecture, in the context of his single trip to India, states his plea that in the post-colonial period, there is a rare opportunity to reset the Hindu–Christian relation, drawing on the spiritual resources of each tradition, in an era where political resentments have subsided and Hindus are showing a remarkable openness to Christ and his message.

10 A partial list of lecturers can be found on Wikipedia at https://en.wikipedia.org/wiki/Teape_Lectures.

11 Some readers will also wonder what I mean by "Hindu" and "Christian." We know that today these labels are hotly contested. "Hinduism" in particular has very often been taken to stand in for a vast array of traditions vaguely connected to one another. While I appreciate the difficulty, and in my own scholarly work do not make much use of "Hinduism" as a word or concept, I have found it necessary to pair "the Christian" with an "Other" in dialogues and projects such as this one.

12 Clothey 1996: 42.

13 Schouten 2008: 260.

14 The *Journal for Hindu–Christian Studies* (and the previous *Bulletin*) is a key site for reflection on the field, and for best examples of individual and collegial work that contributes to the practice and definition of Hindu–Christian studies. Of particular interest are articles that explicitly problematize the nature of Hindu–Christian studies, for example these essays in the 2008 (volume 21) issue: Harold Coward, "A Retrospective of Hindu–Christian Studies: Establishment of the Journal and Formation of the Society"; T. S. Rukmani, "Methodological Approaches to Hindu–Christian

Studies: Some Thoughts"; and Kristin Bloomer, "Comparative Theology, Comparative Religion, and Hindu–Christian Studies: Ethnography as Method." Still earlier, we find similarly informative essays, such as Margaret Chatterjee's "The Prospect for Hindu–Christian Interaction" (1989).

15 Bhabha 1994: 54.
16 Ibid.
17 Ibid., 55.
18 Ibid.
19 Schreiter 1997: 26, cited in Baker 2007: 140–141.
20 Winkler in Clooney 2014: 18.
21 Ibid.
22 Clooney 2015: 7–8.

Lecture One

The Jesuit study of Hinduism

An admirable and imperfect model for Hindu–Christian studies

In this first lecture, I discuss the Jesuit study of Hinduism, to illustrate the possibilities and problems inscribed in the Christian study of Hinduism from the beginning until now. It is just one example, of course, but I draw upon it because the Jesuit tradition of learning is long familiar to me and aptly illustrates how Christians from the West have studied, learned from, and used to their own purposes the Hindu traditions. This Jesuit learning was and is a grand intellectual endeavor, reaching at least from the time of Roberto de Nobili in the 17th century to 18th-century proto-Indologists, to the extraordinary work of the early 20th-century Calcutta Jesuits, and then finally to more recent Jesuits, largely Indian, who have taken the lead in the Jesuit study of Hinduism over the past few decades. This Jesuit project was given a substantial coherence by the identity, beliefs, and policies of the Jesuit intellectual and spiritual path, particularly its confidence in the universality of reason and the productivity of reasoning across religious boundaries.

To study this Jesuit tradition affords insight into the vitality but also the fragility of the Christian study of Hinduism still more broadly: intellectual vigor and impressive curiosity; missionary fervor; focused yet (overly) selective learning; insufficient mutuality; and reliance on expertise and elite conversations. Yet while this Jesuit scholarship was insightful and pioneering in study across religious borders, by our standards and the available historical evidence it was not sufficiently receptive and open to learning from Hindus in an interactive fashion that models the fairness we expect today. This Jesuit learning therefore does *not* model perfectly what we should mean now when we talk about Hindu–Christian studies. But neither is the mix of faith and learning that the Jesuit scholars represent something we ought casually to put aside.

The proto-Indologists and the quest to distinguish culture from superstition

Roberto de Nobili

It is no surprise that I first consider Roberto de Nobili (1579–1656), the pioneering missionary scholar who lived for fifty years in south India. He experimented with adaptation to Indian ways of dressing and living, learned Tamil, and committed himself to substantial study of the religious traditions of Tamil Nadu, both the ideas and the practices. Though he was not the first Jesuit to learn something of Hinduism, he was a great pioneer in deeper and more pointed learning, thus in a way promoting a dimension of what would later on become the Catholic study of Hinduism and, through missionary apologetics, a start on Hindu–Christian dialogue. Because conversions are crucial, he argued that cultural accommodation was justified; he was also witness to the importance of study, and the importance of a way of living conducive to intellectual exchange, lest learning lack depth and endurance. And so he went to extraordinary lengths to adapt to Indian culture, live consonantly with it, and learn the needed languages. De Nobili thought that the Christianity in India must become as culturally, humanly Indian as possible. This signals a key value that we will return to throughout; this is about the fashioning of a space – human, cultural, spiritual – in which substantive religious encounter could take place. Since he was a missionary, of course, he saw himself as entering "their" space, rather than stepping into a new and shared space belonging fully to neither tradition. His intensive engagement with the culture he encountered in India is admirable even from the distance of four centuries, even if his learning – polemical in tone, and one-sided because we have not learned much of his actual interlocutors – is not the ideal for us today.

In several of his Latin treatises – for example, his *Apology* (c. 1610) and *Report on Indian Customs* (c. 1615) – he defends the integrity of Indian culture and the legitimacy of treating it with the same respect afforded to the cultures of ancient Rome and Greece. In the opening of the *Report*, he puts truth in the central place, seeking a fair judgment from all neutral, fair-minded observers:

> It is of the very nature of truth that the more closely it is examined with all fidelity and sympathy, the more splendidly does it shine forth, and the more firmly grounded it proves itself to be in the eyes of judicious investigators.

Accordingly, he says that he has been "examining anew and with perseverance," "the truth of those statements which bear on the customs of this country."[1] He has a truth he wants to communicate, and, paradoxically, the idea that he possesses it already accentuates rather than diminishes his desire to know India's truth. In this way, he gradually recognizes the differences between culture and religion, so as to facilitate a welcoming embrace of the former.

His hopes are great, but when it comes to actual learning, the strengths and flaws of his approach become more evident. For example, his *Inquiry into the Meaning of "God"* (c. 1610) is presented as a philosophical argument on the perfections necessary to a being reasonably termed the supreme being.[2] The qualities mentioned are plausible, with reference to a first cause who is (1) self-existing, (2) without beginning, (3) without a body, (4) by nature possessed of all good qualities, (5) all-pervasive, and (6) lord of all. In seeing this short list, we can immediately think of Indian philosophical traditions that accept the categories (omnipotence, omnipresence) and others that would argue for a distinction (such as whether corporeality is necessarily a flaw); so de Nobili was on solid ground in proposing a conversation.

Throughout the *Inquiry*, de Nobili never uses explicitly Christian vocabulary, and offers no positive arguments for the Christian God in particular. Perhaps he thought that explicitly Christian references were premature; more likely, he would have thought that there was no need for such specificity, since "God" in God's perfections can be understood by all and, in the long run, will turn out to be none other than the "Christian God." Crucial questions can be resolved simply by clear analysis, prior to religious commitments. The latter part of the treatise takes a rather different turn, showing by an eclectic mix of reports of Hindu mythology and his own eye-witness accounts that Hindu deities in fact cannot possibly be thought to have the six perfections belonging to God. Though he is arguing from what he sees around him, we cannot compare his account of living Hinduism with that of other observers in that precise time or place; given the highly critical way in which he uses his observations and reports against Hinduism, we must be hesitant in accepting his version of things. He is an eager learner, but it is difficult to detect a self-critical dimension in his work that would have rendered him more immediately and deeply able to learn from Hindus. His was an age before Western Christians had scruples about possible one-sided appropriations of other cultures and religions.

The *Inquiry* is a classic instance of missionary apologetics, clear, in its own way logically consistent, but lacking in sympathy for the traditions under consideration and evidently unable to read sympathetically the practices of another tradition. De Nobili of course knows his Christian theology well and he consistently (though by our standards hastily) applies his theological categories to Hinduism, for the sake of a hoped-for reasonable conversation. That his knowledge of Indian culture was partial and piecemeal did not discourage him from judging Indian religion in accord with his settled theological norms. The idea of testing conceptual norms by observations of practice is a defensible idea, but his temerity is great, judging implausible and immoral the religions of India as he observed them, only on the basis of the six criteria and what he personally observed and chose to report.

Some observers, edified by the relative openness of de Nobili and his great predecessor Matteo Ricci (who charted a similar path of enculturation in China) unreservedly praise their Jesuit openness, and their willingness to distance themselves from the hegemonic cultural norms of the European Christendom of the times. Some worried that they had gone too far, mixing Christian truths and practices with those of the heathens, becoming too appreciative of what they were seeing and learning. Others, such as Ines Županov,[3] have studied the rhetoric of de Nobili and his colleagues, highlighting how it catered to the good image of Jesuit learning back in Europe. Today we notice acutely the divided intentions of de Nobili and other missionary scholars. They defended Indian customs in their writings to Europeans in part on the basis of their great learning; in other writings, in the vernacular, they used their learning to attack what they perceived to be core religious beliefs interpreted as errors detachable from the sound basics of the cultures where those errors lay embedded. De Nobili's approach would not work now, but only by close reflection on the delicate balance in his writing can we come to a fair estimate of him and why his achievement is pertinent even today, though also flawed and not the sole key to Hindu–Christian studies. He was neither as open-minded as his admirers claim, nor as closed-minded as others accuse him of being; belief and intellectual curiosity were in tension in his mind and writing. Religiously he was adamant about the singular and exclusive truth of Christian faith, even with its philosophical supports and extensions, but he did have great confidence in the ability of people to reason and learn by way of reasoned arguments and the ensuing debates. If the truth of the Christian faith could be argued on philosophical grounds, as his works seem to insist, this marks an openness to learning; where it breaks down and becomes unviable is of course an important topic for investigation.

Dispelling of Ignorance, possibly from late in de Nobili's life, around 1640, is much longer and more complex than the *Inquiry*, even while keeping the same general frame, reflections on the perfections of God then tested with reference to impressions of lived religion. Whether written by de Nobili or a disciple of his, it similarly criticizes the gods and makes much of the perfections of God as a viable measure by which to judge who is the true God, but shows the development of de Nobili's thought into a more empirical verification of reasoned truths about God. In fifteen chapters *Dispelling Ignorance* explores various perfections of God, each topic marking both a positive theology and also a polemical exclusion of other gods.

The argument is more complex than that of the *Inquiry*, and there are many more attributes of the divine deemed necessary to "God" properly understood: (1) this being (necessarily) exists, and is characterized by (2) oneness, (3) self-existence, (4) a spiritual and non-material nature, (5) omnipresence, (6) beginninglessness, (7) omnipotence, (8) infinite wisdom, (9) perfect intelligence, (10) unerring truth, (11) infinite justice, (12) infinite mercy, (13) happiness, and (14) holiness. One chapter is devoted to each perfection, and in each the author criticizes Hindu deities, which, by his assessment, invariably fail to measure up to the perfection at stake. The arguments are somewhat fluid; usually, it is only in the titles of the chapters that the perfections are named as such. Through the narrative openings to each chapter, we find fuller representations of the cultural frame in which de Nobili and his successors imagined their arguments doing their work.

Dispelling Ignorance displays more knowledge of the local religions than did the earlier *Inquiry*, and it also stresses the value of empirical observation, even by introducing scientific learning regarding the size and make-up of the universe. Here too, though on a different register, right knowledge is utilized to make the case regarding who does, and who doesn't, have proper knowledge of the universe. The appeal to geography and astronomy is deeply intertwined with arguments about the nature of India's *sastra*s (instructive religious scriptures). Hindu beliefs, already scrutinized regarding their logic and assessed regarding differences from Christian belief, could now also be assessed with respect to their adequacy to the new scientific account of the world. Most indigenous learning is ruled out as unscientific, even regarding the natural world. Still more interestingly, operative too is a new dynamic regarding European view of religion, a shift in opinion toward the empirical and the verifiable: a religion that cannot verify its claims does not merit being taken seriously. Of course this trend is not entirely to the benefit of the Jesuits, since soon enough Christianity too will be subjected to scrutiny over evidence for its claims and the coherence of its beliefs and practices.

It is not far from *Dispelling of Ignorance* to the rise of a Jesuit mix of ethnography, anthropology, and science – that is to say, to a discourse about India and about Hinduism, favoring the search for superior knowledge over the earlier apologetic aims. For examples of this shift in intellectual disposition, we turn briefly to two later Jesuit scholars, Jean Venance Bouchet and Gaston-Laurent Coeurdoux. In their works, the missionary agenda is muted, though still operative in a subtler, less visible way. Let us then look briefly at these two Jesuits, who, like de Nobili, may be taken as representative of larger trends.

Jean Venance Bouchet

Jean Venance Bouchet, SJ (1655–1732) was a Jesuit missionary in south India for over forty years, largely in the first decades of the 18th century. In 1687 he had gone to Siam (Thailand) as part of a Jesuit mission, but after a 1688 revolution there, the fourteen Jesuits were ejected from the kingdom. Bouchet was one of just three who, upon reaching Pondicherry in 1689, stayed on to join the French mission there. Bouchet reports that by 1702 he had baptized 20,000 adults and heard 100,000 confessions. From Bouchet's letters, we learn that he led a spartan existence, his eating and drinking marked by an austerity owing both to a paucity of resources and to a determination to live as an ascetic. He was a prominent member of the group of Jesuits known as "pandarasamis," who, in Rajamanickam's words,

> were sufficiently respected and at the same time could deal with all the castes, even with the brahmins, though they could not be their teachers. They did not need to be Sanskrit scholars nor strict vegetarians nor were they obliged to fast every day. They could look after the low castes more easily.[4]

What had been de Nobili's personal adaptive practice had become a standard form of missionary acculturation.

Having settled in, Bouchet studied Indian culture and religion in some depth. He wrote nine substantial letters back to Europe which exemplify the progress he had made in understanding India.[5] Bouchet shows an interest in historical explanations, and was eager to trace Indian religion back to the biblical and Greek pagan worlds. Thus his letter on reincarnation manifests both his staunch missionary attitude, and yet also his growing interest simply in the details of Indian religion. The letter covers several main topics: the Indians and the errors of the ancients; transmigration, attacked even by Francis Xavier; and the similarities of the Greek and Indian beliefs regarding reincarnation, considered in detail and with reference to Indian and Greek sources. He then describes how he uses his knowledge of reincarnation in refuting Hindu beliefs, relying on the rigorous logical thinking found in European philosophical argumentation.

Thus, like de Nobili, but with more of a grasp of the topics at hand, Bouchet described at some length what he had learned regarding Hindu views of rebirth. His understanding is advanced for his era, but he is hardly open to new ideas, since beginning to end he is clear that the Indian notion of rebirth is an error. He thought that it was to his advantage to seize their implausible claims, reusing against Indian beliefs arguments thought to have worked in the early Church. Learning and polemic are in tension in the letter; it is only later on, I suggest, that a greater and greater mass of learning will dampen the enthusiasm for polemic and dull the edge of its argumentation. The strengths and obvious shortcomings of this version of the Christian study of Hinduism are manifest: careful learning, enthusiastic participation in European arguments, some engagement with some willing Indian intellectuals, expectations regarding rational discourse – but without an expectation that his Hindu interlocutors might have ideas and arguments not anticipated earlier on in the West. Resources for the Christian study of Hinduism were accumulating, with considerable spiritual energy driving that study, but without satisfactory evidence of the mutuality required for a Hindu–Christian studies that is more than one-sided.

Gaston-Laurent Coeurdoux

We see a step in the ascendancy of Jesuit Indology in the *Manners and Customs of the Indians* (*Mœurs et Coutumes des Indiens*) (1777) of Gaston-Laurent Coeurdoux (1691–1779). This work shows, by my reading, a deeper rebalancing in the intellectual work, with the sheer work of understanding taking precedence over missionary zeal and polemic. If the *Dispelling of Ignorance* stands in-between, still pursuing the polemical agenda, albeit in a very rationalized, reason-respecting manner, the *Manners* proceeds even by a scientific method further distanced from the expectations of religion; science takes the place of religious argumentation. The *Manners* offers a meticulous description of the life, practices, and beliefs of the brahmin.[6]

In *Manners*[7] Coeurdoux has little to say about the purpose of his research. In the descriptive volume accompanying her edition of the *Manners*, however, Sylvia Murr identifies three sets of reasons for its composition. First, there are the larger purposes of the Society of Jesus, as an intellectual, educational, and missionary order of priests which, under attack and suffering suppression and expulsion, found it useful to find expressed in a coherent document all that had been learned. Second, for a wider audience, Coeurdoux and his fellow Jesuits sought to demonstrate their indisputable expertise regarding the people of India, and to show how Indian ways and beliefs should be properly comprehended, and responded to, within a grand Catholic vision congenial to Jesuit practice. Third, there is also Coeurdoux's straightforward and professional desire for correct knowledge, acquired as it were for its own sake.[8] This seems to be the most enduring of reasons proposed by Murr; in this light, the *Manners* is an early instance of a post-missionary study of Hinduism that was largely an intellectual enterprise without any explicit spiritual purpose.

Coeurdoux's scholarship is open to learning from the other, and the *Manners* manifests a greater professional learning about India. Coeurdoux's conjecture on the origins of the doctrine of rebirth (metempsychosis), for instance, is notable for the sympathy of his insights. He leaves aside invective and suspicions of demonic intrigue in order to discern an underlying better purpose: "Metempsychosis was invented, it seems, only to justify providence, and at least to place after this life, under the guise of reward or punishment, a sort of equality between sin and virtue and what arises from good or evil."[9] He concludes the relatively short chapter with a remarkably charitable and sensitive comment on the ways of the idolaters and a criticism of the increasingly alienated intelligentsia of his own country:

> Idolatry, the special character of which is entirely corrupted by its fables, preserved knowledge of a supreme being, his providence, goodness, justice, a knowledge of the spirituality of our souls and their immortality, as well as the necessity of another life accompanied by sufferings and rewards. These are the principles engraved in the hearts of all humans, recognized as indubitable by the first inhabitants of the earth, and even idolatry has respected them. You impious people who reject them – you are worse than the idolaters themselves![10]

The *Manners* is of course not simply a work of Indology, but it exemplifies a professional turn as it were, a determination to listen more closely to the available facts and to describe them without passing judgment. The work of understanding moves to the fore, perhaps still driven by the hope that explanation will render accessible, and then explain away, that which is explained. Yet given the work's incomplete form and the abrupt ending of the early Jesuit mission in India, we can say that a moment for Hindu–Christian understanding, in terms of what we have in a historical record, slipped away here, as study about Hinduism became the priority by and for scholarly elites other than the Jesuits. Coeurdoux's work can be taken as a new beginning in inter-religious learning, even if the experiment was cut off when the Suppression of the Society of Jesus (finalized in 1773) brought the great first innovative period to an end. The Jesuits who returned to Tamil Nadu in the 1830s seem to have been rather uninterested in either literary engagement or doctrinal dispute; perhaps they were hesitant to arouse controversy of any sort. Hinduism was kept at a distance, walled off from theological and practical influence, and the very idea of mutual illumination became, it seems, a distant ideal. The conditions for learning, now on the Jesuit side too, had been blocked.

What, then, do we learn from de Nobili, Bouchet, and Coeurdoux? Many, myself included, will have a mixed reaction to these and other early Jesuit scholars in India. On the one hand, for their era they produced erudite works, often at the cutting edge of learning about the new cultures encountered in the East. Though negative, they take seriously the ideas encountered, and in their confidence in rationality, they believed that arguments could be made to counter ideas they tried to understand and judged to be in error. They were vigorous scholars, inspired by spiritual motives that cannot be reduced to the imperatives of colonialism. On the other hand, the religious and cultural mismatch was severe, their judgments were far too swift, and they proceeded in such a way as to make mutual learning, though seemingly rationally accessible, elusive. Part of the work of Hindu–Christian studies was being done here, but not enough to ensure that a truly reciprocal learning could take place.

Brahmabandhab Upadhyay and the rebirth of the Jesuit study of Hinduism

A new flourishing of Jesuit scholarship occurred around 1900, with a revival of the Jesuit study of Hinduism that was inspired by the Hindu-Christian intellectual Brahmabandhab Upadhyay (1861–1907), whose life and thought are superbly documented by Julius Lipner in his *Brahmabandhab Upadhyay: The Life and Thought of a Revolutionary* (1999). Upadhyay was a notable public figure and leading intellectual in late 19th-century Bengal. Even after he became a Christian and a Catholic, he remained very much on the edge between Hindu and Christian intellectual and spiritual arenas. He directly engaged the philosophical and theological issues debated between Hindu and Christian intellectuals. In attempting to ground and articulate his new Indian Catholic identity, Upadhyay surprisingly found the intellectual vehicle for his vision of Vedanta in rapprochement with Thomism. In a key chapter, "Light from the East?", Lipner recounts Upadhyay's turn to Vedanta in rapprochement with Thomism, as his intellectual bridge between Christianity and India. The task of philosophy, says Upadhyay, is not to challenge or change Christian revelation but to support, defend, clarify, expound, and develop it, and to show its relevance for life. In the past the philosophy of Aristotle had been adapted – "of course minus its errors" – by "the sovereign intellect of St. Thomas Aquinas," and performed the intellectual service for the "Christianity of the Catholic Church" that Vedanta can provide for Christianity in India. Even if in substance Catholic Christianity is everywhere the same, it must in India undergo transformation in form to be intelligible to the Indian mind.[11]

Upadhyay held that the encounter with Vedanta was a decisive moment in the life of the Church: "The Catholic Church has now finally encountered another brand of philosophy that, though it may contain more errors 'because the Hindu mind is synthetic and speculative, and not analytic and practical,' is still and without question 'superior to the Aristotelian–Thomistic synthesis.'"[12] Even if Vedanta may have been misused for the purpose of the Neo-Vedanta polemic against Christianity, if it is properly understood, it can be of great service to Catholics and Catholic theology. Upadhyay is both sympathetic and critical, as Lipner explains. On the one hand, "the Vedantic desire, again assimilated to Hindu religious aspirations tout court, has sought, from early [post-Samhita] times, to penetrate to the heart of the divine mystery"; on the other, "in trying to attain this impossibly exalted end without the divine sanction of supernatural revelation, it has overreached itself and come to some erroneous conclusions." Yet, "as an expression of the 'natural desire' to know God in himself and as a cumulative attempt to understand the divine mystery in the light of reason it has been unequalled in the annals of philosophical-theological inquiry."[13] Much as Westcott was hoping, around the same time, Upadhyay believed that Hindu wisdom was ready and available for appropriation into an Indian Christian synthesis,[14] on Vedantic rather than Aristotelian foundations. What Upadhyay attempted was

> to articulate the relationship in certain areas between Vedanta and Catholic belief. He ambitioned this not by seeking to implant Christian concepts in Vedantic soil so as to arrive at a genuine

> first-order indigenization of the Christian faith, but rather by constructing more or less exact correspondences between Vedantic ideas and Thomistic ones so that Vedanta in some respects may be seen as a form of crypto-(neo)Thomism and Shankara as St. Thomas in disguise.[15]

Upadhyay's synthesis is deepened, even if not rendered easier, by his alertness to the question of the context in which Christian learning can be taken seriously in India. He saw clearly that a reconfiguration of the Christian life was necessary for both the refounding and consequent flourishing of this new Christian culture. His view of Church history taught him that monasticism would be the ground of conversions, as inspirational, but more importantly as presenting a plausible way of life. As he wrote in 1898, "The European clothes of the Catholic religion should be removed as early as possible. It must put on the Hindu garment to be acceptable to the Hindus." He imagined this in terms that would have been familiar to the earliest Jesuits in India:

> This transformation can be effected only by bands of Indian missionaries preaching the Holy faith in the Vedantic language, holding devotional meetings in the Hindu way and practicing the virtue of poverty conformably to Hindu asceticism. When the Catholic Church in India will be decorated with Hindu vestments, then will our countrymen perceive that she elevates man to the universal kingdom of truth by stooping down to adapt herself to his racial peculiarities.[16]

"Decorated with Hindu vestments" seems hardly a deep adaptation, and "racial peculiarities" hardly an adequate description of anything distinctive to different religious cultures; but in the charged political climate of his times, appearances were very important indeed, and the return to "peculiarities" – we might say "particularities" – was a sound instinct.

Upadhyay notes that monasticism had been the wellspring of much of Christian mysticism in the West, and argues that monastic life is necessary if India is to be "conquered and brought under the redeeming yoke of the Catholic Church."[17] In his vision, which I think is not so martial as the quoted words sound, the ashram is where "Hindu Catholics" are to be trained in monastic life, some to be pure contemplatives, meditating on the truth of Satchidananda,[18] and others to be itinerant preachers to bring the truth of Christ to every corner of India.[19] The work of spiritual deepening, fostered in a shared space authentic to India, would be fruitful in the transformation of society as well. Today, too, our studies must take up questions of place, style, and habits of life, lest even the best-intentioned studies remain alien.

Western Jesuit Indologists of the 20th century

Upadhyay's intellectual synthesis opened a fresh space for Hindu–Christian learning, more distant from European Christians and more accessible to Indian Hindus. It is true that he succeeded only to a limited extent, since the hierarchy found his work suspicious, but he did open the way for a new Jesuit engagement with Hinduism, a renewal of the Jesuit Indological tradition. He was a great influence on William Wallace (1863–1922), who in turn pointed the way taken by a series of Jesuit scholars: Georges Dandoy (1882–1962), Pierre Johanns (1882–1955), and their successors, up to Pierre Fallon (1912–1985), Robert Antoine (1914–1981), and Richard de Smet (1916–1995). We can also mention Sister Sarah Grant (1922–2002), de Smet's student, friend, and collaborator.

Wallace, an Anglican missionary who converted to Catholicism and thereafter became a Jesuit, was deeply affected by Upadhyay. As he tells us in his remarkable *From Evangelical to Catholic by Way of the East*, this Evangelical Anglican missionary to India became dissatisfied with the Anglican mission in Bengal, and took up the study of Hinduism, to seek an alternative way into Indian culture and spirituality; and this inquiry led him to Catholicism and into the Society of Jesus. In his unpublished *Introduction to the Hindoo Philosophy*,[20] he writes about why it is imperative to understand if one wishes to be understood:

> Experience shows what reason might teach, that you cannot make one people understand the thought or spirituality of another people unless it be presented to them in terms of their own mind. But in order to present Christianity to the Hindoos in terms of their mind, you must first know their mind and its way of thinking. This you cannot know without study of the Hindoo thought. So until the missionary body makes a study of the Hindoo thought, and grasps it and makes that thought its own, it is vain to hope to get the Hindoos to understand Christian thought and spirituality.[21]

He complains about fruitlessness accruing to the lack of mutual comprehension between Christian missionaries and Hindus:

> The result of this our presenting of Christianity to them in terms of our mind and not of theirs, is that it has no grip either on their

> mind or heart, for they do not understand it nor does it suit their special circumstances.

Upadhyay, whom he does not name, but quotes, is the rare exception:

> It is rare indeed to find a thoughtful and spiritual man become a convert, but there was one such who came to us some twenty years ago. The following is taken from one of his articles, and shows how such men view the actual state of things in the native Christian community: "How it is that Christianity does not thrive in India? There it stands in a corner, an exotic stunted plant with poor foliage, showing little promise of blossom or none. Conversions are almost nil so far as the Hindoo and Mahometan communities are concerned. There are indeed conversions of famine stricken children, of non-Aryans not within the pale of Hinduism, but these acquisitions are on a very insignificant scale. Even the indirect result of Christian preaching is scarcely perceptible. The material civilisation of the West is leavening our society more than the spiritual principles of the Gospel … ."[22]

It is the West, not the Christian way, that India finds affronting its culture and religions each day.

Wallace agrees with Upadhyay in envisioning a new Christian synthesis in India, again quoting Upadhyay:

> So long as Europeanism is not divorced from Christianity, so long as Christian truths are not formulated through Vedantic thought, so long as the Hindoo social fabric is not recognised as an evolution of the Indian genius to destroy which is to destroy the race, so long as the pastors do not become one with the people in their aspirations, so long as Indians are not given the leading position of teachers; so long Christ and His religion will not even be respected by the educated portion of the Hindoo community.[23]

Wallace sees that the task Upadhyay set for himself was more difficult than the latter realized, and unsurprisingly it falls short of the desired goal. But he proposes to pick up the work, at least as an intellectual project:

> So with a view to helping forward intelligent study of the Hindoo the following work has been written. The plan is simple. The Hindoo philosophy is the philosophy of nature and person just as

> the Scholastic may be called that of materia prima and forma substantialis.[24]

This study, he assures his readers, will not be a waste: "For if the West has a priceless jewel for the East in the Faith of the Son of God, so too has the East a priceless treasure for the West in its thought."[25] Reciprocity becomes crucial, in a way not seen in the writings of the earlier Jesuits, even if they recognized that the rich cultures of India held the key to Christianity's health there. In a way, this former Anglican's vision turns out to mesh with that of that other Anglican intellectual of the same era, Bishop Westcott.

By such insights and by his successful appeals to the Society to train a new generation of Indologists, Wallace paved the way for a new generation of Jesuits ready to pursue the goal of a synthesis of Hindu intellectual systems with Christian theology. Thus came to the fore several new generations of scholars, from Georges Dandoy and Pierre Johanns, up to Pierre Fallon and Richard de Smet.[26] Most important is Johann's contribution in "To Christ through the Vedanta," the series of essays published by Johanns with Dandoy in the periodical *The Light of the East*.[27] These small pieces focused on one or another theme in Sankara, Ramanuja, Madhva, Nimbarka, or Vallabha. Johanns, immersed in his studies, rarely backs up to remind readers what he is seeking to do. Although he strongly believed in the fulfillment of Hinduism in Christ, in his writing, as de Smet puts it, "there is no reference to an evolutionary scale of religions or to a surrender of Hinduism to Christianity."[28] Rather, his

> encounter with the Vedantins takes place on the level of philosophy. It develops as a contribution towards a reconciliation of the opposed schools of Vedanta in the light of Thomism, which has the advantage of having synthesized many positive doctrines and being open to assimilating complementary truths.[29]

For Johanns, "positive doctrines" are those "experiential insights" which do not "contradict other experiential insights," but rather "enter with them into a truly rational synthesis."[30] Each Vedantic system is possessed of truths, which, however, require synthesis within and the fully adequate and comprehensive system that is Thomism. Earlier, Johanns had put it this way:

> If the Vedantic philosophers will only bring their several positive statements into harmony, if they will only adjust and thus partially

> limit their assertions, they will turn disconnected doctrines into a system, and that system will be Thomism, or something akin to Thomism.[31]

While "the Vedantins are not requested to adopt Thomism," they are invited "to reconcile their oppositions and, like the Thomists, to pursue in greater harmony their quest for the fullness of truth which stands beyond the reach of philosophy but within the scope of its commanding desire." Although the work of the Calcutta Jesuits was received respectfully and favorably by some Hindus, its primary contribution was to a renewed Catholic consciousness. It affirmed both the truth of the Christian faith and the truths of other faiths. Christianity uplifts and fulfills, rather than destroys, its Hindu others. Theological rigor was meant to pave the way for the spiritual rapprochement necessary to Christian mission in India. In the end, both Vedanta and Thomism must surrender, not to rival philosophical systems, "but in religious faith to the fulfilling Christ who belongs to no man or nation but is of God for all men."[32] This obviously is a bold move to make, and a controversial one. The intellectual efficacy of Thomism smoothly shifts over to that of "the fulfilling Christ," a religious truth now made more easily available due to the clearing of intellectual barriers and misunderstandings by Thomistic analysis. And yet, while we should have reservations about Thomism and about Johanns' seemingly innocent expectation that Hindus will take favorably to seeing Vedanta as fulfilled in a Thomistic synthesis, we must credit him with expressing his views in an intellectually accessible way that allows for response and argument.

Richard de Smet himself was among the last of the foreign Jesuit scholars, and thus the end of the "Upadhyay" line. In a long career, he balanced the study of Vedanta, teaching the religions of India in the Jesuit Jnana Deepa Vidyapeeth and the papal seminary in Pune, and actively participating in dialogue circles throughout India. "The Theological Method of Sankara," his 1953 doctoral dissertation in Rome, has enduring value as pioneering a theological and not simply Indological or philosophical engagement with Sankara. But criticisms still arise. In a critical but not dismissive response to this Calcutta Jesuit stream of learning, Hindu scholar T. S. Rukmani charges that, in his eagerness to find common ground, de Smet does not sufficiently respect differences. Despite his considerable knowledge of Vedanta, she says, he still "has not been able to make a case for either the personhood of Sankara's Advaita Brahman, nor for the origin of the seen universe, both of which differs radically from the Christian God and from creation ex nihilo."[33] His search for parallels failed, since "he was dealing with two entirely different systems of thought."[34] Selective quotations may give the illusion of commonality, but a study of the whole makes commonality far less likely: "Just as in the understanding of Christianity one has to look at all the aspects of its theology, so also, in order to correctly comprehend Advaita, it is necessary to read Sankara's commentaries as a whole in order to arrive at an understanding of Advaita in all its dimensions. Selective use of a line here or there" does not lead to a comprehensive understanding.[35] Stressing that she does not mean to dishonor de Smet, Rukmani rightly insists that new interpretations "have to be in conformity with the understanding of the scholar they seek to interpret."[36] De Smet, of course, spent his career trying to do just that, and is hardly a dilettante merely quoting "a line here or there."

More controversially, but in a way that helps illumine what is at stake here, Rukmani proposes that only purely non-prejudiced scholarship – admittedly impossible – would be truly fair to the traditions studied. After acknowledging, indebted to Hans-Georg Gadamer, that prejudice is inevitable, she seems disappointed that de Smet did not achieve an entirely neutral consciousness, and so fell short of the perfect Hindu–Christian intellectual rapprochement she demands:

> Dr. De Smet was a Christian theologian and though sincere in his approach to Sankara and in his efforts to understand Sankara's Advaita Vedanta, could not rid himself of his 'prejudices.' His efforts, therefore, to reinterpret Brahman, tadatmya, adhyasa, and other Sankarian terms and concepts, in order to bring Sankara's Advaita closer to Christian theology, have not yielded the desired result, in my view.[37]

But more leeway is required here. Perfection, however noble an ideal, can be the enemy of the good. It is wiser to say this differently: to see learning as a means merely of confirming one's own positions, or to disregard it as merely neutral, would be inimical to religious and interreligious learning; and so we must be imperfectionists, so to speak. Imperfect study and learning must be welcomed, provided bias is candidly admitted and correction welcomed, lest we thwart Hindu–Christian learning by holding only to the highest standards of perfection.[38]

For Johanns and his collaborators in the "To Christ through the Vedanta" series, and more temperately for successors such as de Smet, the individual truths, gaps, and distortions found in the basically sound Vedanta traditions could be rectified by integration into the comprehensive system that is Thomism, possessed as it is with realistic and harmonious understandings of God, world, and human being. This intellectual integration and energy differed greatly from that of de Nobili and other earlier Jesuits, and marked a great shift in how the Jesuit scholars perceived their work. Gone from the writings of this group at least were polemics against Hindu idolatry and darkness, absurdity and self-contradiction. Confidence in the superiority of the Thomistic synthesis remained robust, as a kind of intellectual stand-in for the older religious polemics. But the door was opened to a different kind of exchange, such as de Smet yearned for and Rukmani obliquely shows us in her rejoinder to him: an honest argument among collegial equals.

The contribution of Indian Jesuit scholars

As the number of foreign Jesuits in India declined, the Indological work was taken up Indian Jesuit Indologists, including, in the older generation, Mariasusai Dhavamony (1925–2014), Ignatius Puthiadam (1930–), and John Vattanky (1931–). These scholars, diligent and steady, built on the work of European Indologists in a professional way.

Mariasusai Dhavamony, a scholar of religion in south India and a professor in Rome, was more explicit on the theological issues, though perhaps without integrating his Indology and his theology. He wrote widely on themes in missiology, theology of religions, dialogue, and related fields. He is best known for his *Love of God according to Saiva Siddhanta* (1971), a very useful survey of the theme of devotion in the Siddhanta. His work thus proceeds on two tracks: on the one hand, expert and fair studies in the works of south Indian Hindu figures, ranging from Sankara and Ramanuja to various Tamil saints, and on the other, a traditionalist and cautious reading of Vatican II regarding the religions. Other than positing, without explanation, that "Saiva Siddhanta, no doubt, represents the high level of India's deeply religious experience,"[39] he remains neutral, and does not step back and question his own clearly Christian perspective. However, in other writings, he clearly ranks "the religions" as lower than Christianity. In "Evangelization and Dialogue" (1989), he writes, "Religions are said to be incomplete searches for God. They cannot establish an authentic and living relationship with God." Yet this does not necessarily mean that they are "merely natural expressions without a supernatural element in them." That their scriptures have a role to play is indubitable, and these religions hold "a splendid patrimony of religious writings … that have taught generations of men how to pray" – though how inspiration plays a role is "left to the study and reflection of the theologians."[40]

The short essay then goes on to criticize Rahner's anonymous Christianity concept. Nowhere does Dhavamony draw on his expertise in the literature of devotion in India to make a more grounded case against Rahner. Conversely, his two 1988 essays on Ramanuja and Sankara, "Sankara as a Commentator on Hindu Scriptures" and "Ramanuja as Interpreter of the Hindu Scriptures," make no reference to Church documents, Vatican II, or related matters.[41] It is as if there were two separate compartments to his scholarship, each weaker in the absence of the other.

Ignatius Puthiadam studied in Germany and became a scholar of dualist Vedanta, producing a dissertation on Madhva, *Gott, Welt und Mensch bei Madhva* (1975), and in English, *Visnu, the Ever Free: A Study of the Madhva Concept of God* (1985). Some of his work is more explicitly comparative, for example, *God in the Thought of St. Thomas Aquinas and Sri Madhvacarya* (1978–1989), his University of Madras lectures on Madhva and Aquinas. In such works, the value of the study is largely taken to be self-evident, the topic of God treated as of self-explanatory importance, and comparison not in need of defense. The case is not made why and how this expert study might affect how Christians are to think of God. It is only in other works, dedicated to the realities and practices of dialogue, that Puthiadam became more explicit regarding the rationale for his work in a multi-religious India. Certainly, he is exemplary in trying to do both the study and the creation of new venues for learning. John Vattanky was another accomplished scholar. He studied at Oxford and in Vienna, and was perhaps the first Jesuit to study Nyaya in depth, leading to some impressive scholarly publications, such as his *Ganesa's Philosophy of God* (1984). But in that writing, as far as I can see, he did not explain why he did this very difficult work on Hindu logic, nor did he indicate how it might affect Jesuit and Catholic intellectual life in India.

Just a few of the (now senior) scholars of the next generation can also be mentioned. Francis X. D'Sa has written voluminously as an Indologist (see his *Sabdapramanyam in Sabara and Kumarila*, 1980), and by way of comparative theological works: He thus offers a range of readings, from the Indological to the dialogical, with attention to the doctrinal substance of commonalities connecting the Hindu and Christian traditions. His *Gott der Dreieine und der All-Ganze: Vorwort zur Begegnung zwischen Christentum und Hinduismus* (1987) is an impressive, sophisticated work that seeks to think through in a comprehensive way the encounter of Hinduism and Christianity. He first offers a theological apprehension of each tradition, in terms of core beliefs grounded in scripture and expressed in relation to cosmic and ethical implications. Subsequent chapters compare and contrast cosmo- and anthropo-centric worldviews, Trinity and the Totality, prayer and meditation, "inspired scripture and 'exspired' sruti," the Pentecost giving of the Spirit, and liberation. He proposes an "intercultural theology" which proceeds by the holistic engagement the book itself exemplifies: not a single word or theme, but an overall consideration of the two traditions "next to" one another, as religious cultures – and thus in a way in harmony with what we hope for in Hindu–Christian studies.

Anand Amaladass is a respected Sanskritist, widely published author, translator, and editor of thematic volumes. He has also turned toward the arts, undertaking other projects, including a volume of Indian Christian hymns and, with Gudrun Löwner, the impressive *Christian Themes in Indian Art* (2012). Amaladass too seems less optimistic on how this learning might fit into the overall formation of Jesuits, and thus change how theology and philosophy were to be done. Though he does not write extensively about Hindu–Christian relations, in "Viewpoints: Hindu–Christian Dialogue Today" (1997) he surveys the challenges facing the field and comments on the difficulties in Hindu–Christian exchange, including persistent Hindu doubts about Christian intentions, but notes also that changes in each tradition and in Indian society as a whole promise new ways of encounter. He concludes with a hopeful observation:

> One cannot measure the Hindu–Christian dialogue in terms of numbers (of meetings, publications, or subscriptions to related journals) but by perceiving the growing awareness of one another's presence in public life; and the challenge it offers to re-think about one's own religious tradition with reference to others is already a great achievement.[42]

Noel Sheth, a third distinguished scholar, is widely published and has lectured globally. He sees his work as both Indological and comparative. Some of his writing is strictly Indological, as he brings a good historical and theological sense of readings of the narratives of Rama and Krishna, for instance, with a good eye to what is most significant. His comparative work draws Christian and Hindu texts, beliefs, and doctrines into comparison, so as to discover both similarities and differences; he is confident that by comparison, each side in the Hindu–Christian conversation will learn more about themselves and see also how the other tradition enriches and complements one's own. Because he is a perceptive theologian as well as a trained Sanskritist, he can propose more mature and constructive comparisons with subtler theological categories in play, having put aside false views and stereotypes of the other. A good example of his work in this regard is the 2002 article "Hindu *Avatara* and Christian Incarnation: A Comparison." The main part of the essay offers careful expositions of a number of Hindu views of *avatara*, and Christian views of incarnation, with attention to differences within the traditions, and how those differences are to be weighed. In turn, those detailed descriptions allow for far more fine-tuned philosophical, theological, and ethical comparison than usually emerges; neither tradition is held up as without problems, yet both are respected by Sheth's effort at true understanding. The overall comparative point of the essay is previewed at its start, when Sheth affirms that "comparison not only facilitates better mutual understanding but also helps each tradition to understand itself better." Through comparison and contrast "a faith can come to comprehend itself more deeply"; similarities "help us to appreciate the larger significance of our beliefs and practices," while "differences give us insights into the unique features of our own tradition."[43] As for the resultant "cross-cultural fertilization" that occurs, Sheth remarks, at the essay's end, that the compared "original elements may themselves undergo transformation and acquire new meaning and significance" beyond the understandings proposed within the tradition thus far.[44] Had this view become deeply imbedded in the Catholic consciousness, or even more simply normative in Jesuit seminary education, Hindu–Christian studies would have gained by now a firmer basis.

I could continue naming even younger Jesuit intellectuals, but I hope that such indications suffice to make clear that the transition to Indian Jesuit Indology did not mark any decline, but perhaps an increase in the quality of Indological research, in the work of these figures. By my reading, all these Jesuit scholars of the 20th and 21st centuries, some foreign and some Indian, have made a distinctive contribution in their recalculation of how Indology matters. The more recent figures became less concerned about metaphysical foundations in Thomism, even as they were less concerned about conversions. In light of Vatican II, perhaps, they sought to reframe the Christian engagement with Hinduism as a kind of interreligious dialogue. But as a result, such work seems to have been treated simply as a kind of dialogue or aid to dialogue – if one wanted to dialogue with brahmins – and not pertinent to the transformation of Catholic consciousness through learning from the Hindu traditions. The Hindu other was not taken seriously enough to effect a real change in the Christian heart. This made it easier for dioceses, seminaries, and mainstream theological writing to overlook work in this area, or to turn away from it when the initial optimism for dialogue had waned. Consequently, as we shall see below, the recalculation of Indology as dialogue and *ad extra* made its value depend on the worth of dialogue, in an era when dialogue with brahmins became the subject of great suspicion.

Pushing the Jesuit study of Hinduism to the margins

Despite the excellent work of these Jesuit scholars, Western and Indian, throughout the 20th century and now in the 21st, it has never been certain that the intellectual infrastructure would remain strong enough to ensure that Hindu–Christian learning would become more and not less central to the work of the Jesuits even in India. As in the era of the 18th-century termination of the early Jesuit experiment, even the formidable scholarship of 20th-century Jesuits seems to have lacked sufficiently deep roots and broad appeal to have a hoped-for impact. The seminary structure remained under Vatican supervision, managed from afar, and too often ruled over by those with minimal appreciation for the Hindu–Christian exchange; Thomism lost its grip on Catholic intellectual life; a few Jesuits were scholars, most were not; the active work of dialogue was not balanced by interreligious study integral to Jesuit training or the teaching in Jesuit educational institutions. As far as I have been able to see, Indian Jesuit scholars have been more adept in the intellectual work of Indology and direct dialogue than in the task of forming an organic "new Catholic scholasticism" – perhaps because the narrative of mission, even as undergirding the Indian Christian scholarship, is insufficient to undergird the self-understanding of Indian Jesuit scholars, such as would more deeply transform Christian identity in light of learning from Hinduism. The learning of some Jesuits about Hinduism was formidable, but the overall integration of that learning into Jesuit learning and life had fallen short; it may be that the Jesuit tradition of the study of Hinduism was not deep enough to survive at the onset of new concerns of a rather contrary sort.

As a result, when new energies came to the fore in Catholic India, most notably in the rise of liberation theology and Dalit theology, the Jesuit scholars seem not to have persuasively made the case why such learning, especially learning from brahmins, was still worthwhile. The learning was pushed to the side and formalized largely in elective courses in seminaries. When the Jesuit study of Hinduism ceased to be central enough to most Jesuits' consciousness, it also became much less likely to endure after the practical turn to liberation theology. The great Jesuit tradition was marginalized, even among Jesuits. Instead of Christian intellectuals arguing for interreligious studies on spiritual and intellectual grounds, the debate occurred largely on more practical grounds. Most Jesuits simply continued the work of schools and social ministries; proponents of more radical social action argued with proponents of the spiritual acculturation evident in Christian ashrams. The "pure scholars" of Indological studies were pushed to the side by those impatient with the slow pace and modest accomplishments of scholarship, while others, Jesuit and Catholic as well as Hindu, chose to read Hindu–Christian exchange only through the dour and even jaundiced perspective of political motivations and power dynamics. The debate over enculturation was instead pursued in arguments between the new activists and stalwart proponents of Christian ashrams, who argued for the enduring necessity of shared contemplative spaces where Hindus and Christians could meet, learn, and pray together.[45] In the end, there was not enough shared space among Catholics themselves, much less in intellectual and spiritual communion with Hindus, for a Hindu–Christian intellectual exchange to thrive.

Much more would have to be said to fill out a complete picture of the Western and Indian Christian engagement with Hinduism, of course. But my main point in this lecture has been to highlight the fragility and rarity of the mix of curiosity and humility, groundedness and openness, that marks a fruitful study of the Other, if such study is to be interreligiously productive, generative, and sturdy enough to survive the push-back of different or even alien concerns. The Jesuit tradition was and is impressive indeed, but cannot of itself be the model for interreligious learning, not only because of its evangelical motive for much of its history, but also because it did not seek or find a common ground on which to engage Hindus in true and equal exchange. Particularly in the 20th century, the intention was present, but institutional and historical factors thwarted major success in this area.

We need in any case to keep looking for other, different and complementary instances of Hindu–Christian learning. Specifically, we need to reflect on Hindu examples of learning from the Christian West, by a learning that has been real and enduring, and often enough in search of a common spiritual ground, even if often not expressed in the language of theology. Here too, there is a long history, for Hindus have studied the West, though not with the theological expertise one might hope for. This is the topic of Lecture Two.

Notes

1 De Nobili 2000b [c. 1615]: 53.
2 De Nobili 2000a [c. 1610].

3 See Županov 1999.
4 Rajamanickam 1972: 49.
5 See Clooney 2005a.
6 Here is a brief overview of the themes of the fifty-two chapters, drawing on Murr's (1987) outline: 1–5, on caste; 6–9, on brahmins; 11–16, on the student stage of life (*brahmachari*); 17–38, on the life and customs of the householder (*grhastha*); 39, on forest-dwelling (*vanaprastha*); 40–43, on the fourth stage, that of the renunciant (*sannyasi*); 44–49, on related topics: deities, rebirth, sciences, myths and moral tales, scriptures; 50, on the pariah caste; 51, on the military customs; 52, on the geography of India.
7 In the manuscript as we have it according to Sylvia Murr (ibid.).
8 The preceding paragraphs are based on ibid., vol. II: 56–64.
9 Coeurdoux, SJ, found in ibid., vol. I: 142.
10 Ibid., vol. I, 144.
11 Lipner 1999: 186. For an excellent review of the engagement of Thomism and Indian thought from Upadhyay to the present, see Ganeri 2015.
12 Lipner 1999: 186.
13 Ibid., 186–187.
14 Lipner comments that this is a "remarkable re-evaluation of Vedanta," even if it is based on "a virtually absolute compartmentalization between the insights of the 'natural' light of reason and supernatural revelation" (ibid.: 187).
15 Ibid., 188. Interestingly, Lipner admits (ibid.,189) that Upadhyay's turn to Vedanta in this particular way is a bit of a puzzle, never fully explained.
16 Bangalore 2002: 207.
17 Ibid., 202.
18 Ibid., 208.
19 Ibid., 203.
20 Excerpts from unpublished typescript by William Wallace, SJ, "An Introduction to the Hindoo Philosophy," dated October 16, 1909, and archived at the Goethals Library, St. Xavier's, Kolkata. I am grateful to my student, Chen Rao, for photographing these pages for me.
21 Ibid., 4.
22 Ibid., 4–5.
23 Ibid., 5–6.
24 Ibid., 6.
25 Ibid.
26 For instance, Richard de Smet, SJ writes: "We have patiently followed up the direction pointed out to us by Upadhyaya towards the great Vedantin and we have discovered a doctrine which, far more than the teachings of the Greek Philosophers, provides an intellectual body for the Christian Spirit. Let us hope that this lead will in the future be followed with more and more decision and let us wait with confidence for the day when the Christian Mysteries will shine more convincingly to everyone in this land in an authentically Indian garb." From an unpublished 1949 text reproduced in de Smet 2013b, p. 462. For a review of key (Western) Catholic thinkers in India indebted to Brahmabandhab, see Lacombe 1951.
27 Ganeri 2015 traces the Jesuit study of Vedanta in the 20th century, and Doyle's *Synthesizing the Vedanta* (2006), a study of Johanns, likewise introduces us to him and other major figures. For our purposes here,

though, Richard de Smet's summation in his essay "Sankara Vedanta and Christian Theology" (2013a) suffices as background for our comments on Johanns.

28 De Smet 2013a: 384.

29 Ibid.

30 Ibid.

31 Johanns 1996: 5–6.

32 De Smet 2013a: 384.

33 Rukmani 2003: 19.

34 Ibid.

35 Ibid.

36 Ibid.

37 Ibid.

38 In a 2008 essay, Rukmani admits that she is "convinced that there is place in the academy for Hindu–Christian studies, as it created space for an in depth exploration of both Hinduism and Christianity in a comparative or exclusive manner" (2008: 43). But having said that, she shifts to another line of critique, insisting on the need to attend to realities on the ground, outside the academy, lest the field be reduced to the study of the past. Even the great texts need to be read in light of their current use since, Rukmani says, "religion is what religion does" (ibid., 45) True enough; but there is truth too in a counterbalancing view, that what religions say about themselves, even in refined doctrine, forms a valuable measure of and corrective to even the most popular of current practices. Without grounded theological learning, even the issues of urgent current interest – conversions, caste, etc. – can be easily misread in a too-hasty take on the issues.

39 Dhavamony 1971: 378.

40 Dhavamony 1989: 279.

41 Respectively, pp. 141–164 and 165–189 in Dhavamony 1988.

42 Amaladass 1997: 42.

43 Sheth 2002: 98.

44 Ibid., 115.

45 On the liberationist critique of the study of Hinduism and of Christian ashram life as well, see Soares-Prabhu 1991, Grant and Amalraji 1993, and Gravend-Tirole 2014.

Lecture Two

How (and why) some Hindus have studied Christianity

In this second lecture, I turn toward the Hindu reception of Western and Christian traditions, in order to see the possibilities and limitations of Hindu–Christian studies in light of Hindu intellectual work. Today we must pay closer attention to the considerable Hindu efforts to engage the Christian West without confining such efforts within conceptual frames arising in the West.

This subject is not precisely symmetrical with that of the first lecture, since Hindus and Christians have never faced exactly the same problems in the study of each other's intellectual and spiritual traditions. Christians have largely been in a position to decide whether and when such learning is worthwhile, and Hindus have often been compelled, socially and intellectually, to acknowledge and respond to questions and challenges posed by the West. Tinu Ruparell has aptly noted that many Hindus he spoke with "are not interested in discussing with Christians their respective views of God and the transcendent." While we "might expect Hindus, of all people, to be most keen to debate the finer points of theology with any and all people of faith," in fact that learning is too often a tainted gift, burdened with a difficult history and carrying "unfortunate connotations." It can seem a residual tool of empire, or an instrument of evangelization, best responded to by indifference and silence rather than trusting participation. Engaging in interreligious dialogue with Christians may reopen the door "to an imperial history many Hindus wish to leave behind. Just how much this explains Hindu reticence to partake in dialogue with Christians may be debated." Efforts to reset Hindu–Christian studies as a more fruitful discipline must from the start respect differences, repent for histories of violence, respect the considerable learning from and about the West that Hindus have already undertaken, and take into account how Hindu religious intellectuals have chosen to engage the West.[1]

Hindus have never studied Christianity in the way Christians have studied Hinduism, nor would we want to expect them to; and so we must be on the lookout for other forms of substantive learning, perhaps under other names. The intellectual background and resources of Indian traditions diverge greatly and interestingly from those of the premodern and modern West; motives and methods have varied, and Christian and Western expectations have often been disappointed when the study does not proceed as expected. Nonetheless, the presupposition of this lecture is that Hindu intellectuals have indeed engaged in serious study of Western and Western Christian ideas. There is a great abundance of evidence, if we know where to look and do not restrict ourselves to dialogues or theological exchanges. Some Hindu intellectuals have gone to extraordinary lengths in order to study Western philosophy, appropriate it from a Hindu perspective, and fashion parallels to texts of the Hindu and other Indian traditions. Sometimes this study has not fit into the expected academic categories of Western scholarship, and thus been ignored. But even then it often and impressively holds together the intellectual and spiritual realms – in a way that Christian scholarship has not always done – and created a common ground for some Hindus and Christians to engage in substantive mutual learning. In the following pages, I highlight just a few instances where learning was substantive and constructive, and not merely in reaction to or defense against Christian initiatives.

Two pioneering figures in scholarly exchange

Algondavilli Govindacharya

The first author I wish to introduce in this very selective survey is Algondavilli Govindacharya (c. 1860–1940).[2] If remembered today, it is generally for his still useful writings on the Srivaisnava tradition, *The Divine Wisdom of the Dravida Saints* (1902a) and *The Holy Lives of the Alvars* (1902b). His later *Mazdaism in the Light of Vishnuism* (1913) is an explicitly comparative study that shows the curiosity and inquisitiveness of this Srivaisnava scholar. What distinguishes such works is their impressively specific and insightful knowledge of Western thought – biblical, Christian spiritual, and philosophical – and consistency in identifying specific points of similarity or difference. Well versed on both sides of the matters at hand, Govindacharya was the rare scholar who could engage in a learning that in the end was indebted to both of the traditions involved, but reduced to neither.

Throughout his career, his larger agenda was to think through basic truths and methods of inquiry in Hinduism and Christianity, with an eye toward finding common ground for the conversation between the traditions. Of particular interest are his *Three Lectures on Inspiration, Intuition, and Ecstasy* (1897).[3] These lectures are among his earlier works and thus predictive of key themes in his later writing. The first deals with the philosophical and religious traditions of the West, the second with those of India, and the third largely with theosophy as a wisdom arising in both the East and the West, and thus, he hopes, serving as a bridge between the two worlds.[4] His aim is a universally available, albeit hidden, wisdom that comes "not from one, but from many, sources." He hopes to show that "inspired or revealed knowledge is the source which partly, if not wholly, unveils the underlying power behind phenomena."[5] For the sake of a rational exposition of this project, he soberly notes and weighs various means of access to divine insights, and estimates the success or failure of religious thinkers, philosophers and theologians, in holding together rational and intuitive modes of learning.

In his introduction to the lectures, Govindacharya introduces the major concepts that together undergird a way of knowing that goes beyond ordinary objective and subjective learning:

> In an inquiry on *inspiration* thus, we have necessarily to consider what is known as revelations, and what is known as *intuitional* knowledge; and the experiences known as ecstasies and visions, etc., and knowledge which is called divine illumination, all forming subjects of collateral importance. We shall also be led to an inquiry as to what *intuition* is meant by the eclectic philosophers of the day, the Brahma-Samajists, etc., and how it is connected with *inspiration*.[6]

In the first lecture Govindacharya explores some Greek sources, particularly Plato and Plotinus, and then Christian sources, from the Bible to Teresa of Ávila, Emanuel Swedenborg, and more recent figures, in order to present evidence for an ancient and long-term Western and Christian appreciation of what is at stake: a balance between revelation mediated through scripture, studied in terms of reason, and alternate means of inspiration and ecstasy. Govindacharya is generous in his descriptions, but does not hesitate to be critical of what he considers Christianity's over-institutionalization. For example, near the end of the first lecture, he encourages the search for a common ground outside the dogmatic tradition and in a retrieval of the ancient wisdom traditions:

> When the Bible is full of such experiences [of visions and ecstasies], that Faith alone should be insisted on, as the final criterium, divorcing Philosophy on one side, and spurning Intuition on the other, is decided unreason. Unless Christianity can be reconstructed both on Faith and on Philosophy somewhat after the old Alexandrian model,[7] it will never adapt itself to the complete nature of man.

He offers a specific criticism of the Christian synthesis that overly promotes and protects faith: it

> can never cope with the philosophical or metaphysical methods to which Vedantism has accustomed the Indian intellect. Put the Bible before the Vedantin, and he at once asks for a proper explanation of the nature of body, of soul and of God, and the relation in which they stand to each other, etc.; but such explanation as his philosophical bias demands does not exist in the Bible.[8]

Some other ground, more capacious and inclusive of the experiential, yet not reductive, must be found. Govindacharya then concludes specifically to the value of combining this return to the experiential and metaphysical with new interreligious learning, to bring out the best in the Christian: "Not only then, that Christianity has to reconstruct on the Alexandrian basis, but it has to enrich itself from the spiritual treasures abundantly to be found in the Revelations of the East."[9] After some further comments on the ecstatic experience of St. Augustine, and on modern psychology and the recognition of sudden, unexpected moments of insight, at the end he offers this expansive vision: "there is in man potencies and possibilities beyond the bounds limited by his present knowledge."[10]

Govindacharya's second lecture deals with the same questions arising in the religions of India. He inquires into the interplay of knowledge, experience, and intuition as seen in the Upanisads, the *sutra* texts of Yoga, Vedanta and the other philosophical systems (*darsanas*), and in the writings of Keshab Chunder Sen, Vivekananda, and others who, like himself, sought theosophical wisdom. He is seeking after signs of growth in God-consciousness, though distinguishing more developed and introspective models. Key once again is intuitional knowledge that grows toward that higher realization[11] that is the essence of true religion. Govindacharya cites Vivekananda on the yoga: "According to [the teachers of yoga], the only proof of the Scriptures is that they were the testimony of competent persons, yet they say, the Scriptures cannot take us to realization."[12] He then reemphasizes the main point:

> realization is real religion, and all the rest is only preparation – hearing lectures, or reading books, or reasoning, is merely preparing the ground; it is not religion. Intellectual assent, and intellectual dissent, are not religion. The central idea of the yogis is that just as we come in direct contact with objects of the senses, so religion even can be directly perceived in a far more intense sense.[13]

At stake for Govindacharya is a manner of intuition that is irreducible to any religion's sacred books or authorized revelations, but nevertheless available in those religions and, if the religions are read properly, is available to all advancing along the spiritual path. He admits the danger of subjectivism – a privatization apart from the religions – but insists that the capacious wisdom of God can include all the religious paths and every individual.[14] He then offers testimonies from various scriptures and from contemporary European theorists of psychology, in order to highlight the fact and importance of ecstatic, intuitional consciousness. Much space is given over to testimonies from the Hindu scriptures on this higher consciousness. Later he argues with Brahmo Samaj, including Keshab Chunder Sen, on the hope for rational criteria for discovering the truth in religions. If there is no underlying intuitive power, he says, we will end up with no scriptures and no authorities, but only merely subjective guesses as to what is true and enduring.[15] Intuition is not opposed to revelation, but is its source and the best route to identifying it.[16]

The goal of the first two lectures was to consider in some depth issues related to the intersection of the divine and human, the mind and spirit, in order to establish by comparison that there dispositions and instincts, in each tradition, that would facilitate a rapprochement of the traditions. Near the end of the second lecture, Govindacharya traces the themes running through both:

> I have shown how Indian philosophers discovered one truth or another, stated in some form or other, out of their intuitional depths, and how intuitions become inspirations when men utter them who are known to be saints or God-sent men. I have shown what Revelations are – and how they are connected with inspiration and ecstasy. I have shown the relative importance of the senses, the understanding, and the innate intuitive faculty of man, as sources of knowledge. I have shown the importance of Inspiration and Revelation as giving us a knowledge of God and spiritual truths beyond the capacity of our ordinary senses to ken, and the

> utmost importance of the Vedas, the Aryan Scriptures. I have shown the controversial differences on these several questions.[17]

At the start of the third lecture, Govindacharya quotes Vivekananda in support of his vision of the complementarity of East and West: "India has to learn from Europe, the conquest of external nature, i.e., of substance, and Europe has to learn from India the conquest of internal nature." He thinks that this mutual learning will open up new possibilities, for what amounts to an ideal third space:

> Then there will be neither Hindus nor Europeans – there will be the ideal humanity which has conquered both natures, external and internal. We have developed one phase of humanity and they another. It is the union of the two that is wanted.[18]

Granting "the old story" of "innate ideas, intuitional knowledge, inspiration and revelation," he proposes to "enquire a little how this old question re-appears under its latest presentation, Theosophy," which is "the third ray" in his consideration.[19] Here a theosophical vision comes to the fore. He remains candid in his confidence his confidence in the power of Vedanta; without its guidance, Christians will not become again able to understand their own scriptures. Indeed, again quoting Vivekananda, "Vedanta is the *rationale* of all religions. Without Vedanta every religion is superstition," but with it, "everything becomes religion."[20] Yet it is in theosophy that we find a meeting point of India and the West, "since theosophy ought to be considered as not only the flower of Western thought but the realization of the dream of the Indian philosophers from whom the West had already borrowed so much."[21] Through theosophy, one transcends ordinary perception, without losing entirely one's sense of grounding in what is real.[22] He reports,

> H. P. B. [Helena Blavatsky] plainly tells us, that the Vedas are as it were the source of all other Revelations, and that spiritual truths which can be obtained by one's own intuition is in harmony with that found in the Vedas; and the Vedas being the corroborated cumulative testimony of ages of saints, it can safely be trusted as a help to the growth of one's own intuition in the manner of a child in its leading strings till it can walk by itself; or twigs provided as props to a climbing creeper.[23]

This claim is unlikely to convince those not well disposed toward theosophy, to be sure, but it merits our reflection. What is directly interesting is the explicit interplay between personal intuition, the Veda understood as grounded in the intuitions of the sages, and the broader intuitive experiences of the human race.

Govindacharya then makes a further distinction that emphasizes theosophy's grounding in revelation (*sruti*):

> the position taken up by Theosophy is quite distinct from that taken by the Brahma Samajists. Both are eclectic systems, but Theosophy declares that Vedas are trustworthy intuitional knowledge, which when one believes, he is safe enough, and with which his individual intuitions do not collide.

By contrast, the Brahmists are individualists who by the weapon of their "individual intuition" pare down revelation to what fits with their own intuitions, rather than challenging their understanding of intuition by respect for scripture.[24] At least in this version of the matter, theosophy's portrayed respect for Vedic tradition helps us to imagine a correlative respect for Christian revelation and tradition as well. A theologian committed to both faith and reason, Govindacharya asserts that neither reason nor blind faith can discover the truth. Room must be left for instinct and the imagination.[25] At the end of his essay he similarly quotes at length from Annie Besant and then, rather unexpectedly, closes with an exegesis of Brahma Sutras III.3.12–14, as read according to his own Vaisnava tradition.[26] He sees this *sutra* text as proposing the general idea of a supreme God who is specified by several key perfections (bliss, knowledge, purity), who then takes on other attributes for the sake of meditation, geared to the preferences of the meditator's own spiritual instincts. This too contributes to what, in Govindacharya's view, is a fair encounter of India and the West.

Whatever we think of theosophy, faded and exotic to our ears, it is still the case that we ought to appreciate Govindacharya's great erudition, his close attention to both sides of his inclusive and deeply comparative project, and his search for a deep and common space wherein the best of Indian and Western, Hindu and Christian, traditions could meet. He engaged in Hindu–Christian study because he had a view of the world that required such inquiry, if religious and intellectual dilemmas were to be resolved and the goods he hoped for to be gained. Without a space like this, at least presented as a hypothesis, we will hardly be able to get beyond the notion of incommensurable cultures and the preordained failure of any sort of interreligious learning. Instead, we will be thwarted by a host of political issues, concerns about power, and a sheer impossibility of translation and communication, such that any hopes we might have regarding Hindu–Christian learning will be nearly extinguished.[27]

Brajendranath Seal

Brajendranath Seal (1864–1938) was a renowned philosopher, credited with many respected writings. He was a contemporary of Govindacharya, and wrote with a consonant intent, though he eschewed theosophy and instead sought precision in historical knowledge and in method. For my purposes, most remarkable was his venture in comparative philosophy and theology, *Comparative Studies in Vaishnavism and Christianity with an Examination of the Mahabharata Legend about Narada's Pilgrimage to Svetadvipa and an Introduction to the Historico-Comparative Method* (1899). This project of historical retrieval was a pioneering contribution to the emerging field of comparative philosophy in the modern era. In it Seal aims to put comparative studies on a surer footing, so as to clarify and assess – and thus rebalance – the relationships between India and the West, Vaishnavism and Christianity. Early on in the lecture he indicates his desire to avoid the pitfalls of comparative work as he had observed it done previously. He is blunt:

> The comparative method of investigating the sciences relating to the history of the Human Mind requires elucidation and correction, for nothing has done greater mischief in this department of research than the ill-conceived and blundering attempts of so many tyros and "prentice hands" to build ambitious theories and comprehensive systems on the shifting quicksands of loose analogy and vague generalization in the name of scientific method.

For this, he sets out a number of presupposition and rules. He seeks temporal parallels, but avoids asserting that contemporality proves affinity or indebtedness. Proper method must presuppose the equal dignity of the comparands and catch them in parallel moments in their development, since "historical comparison such as is here proposed implies that the objects compared are of co-ordinate rank, and belong more or less to the same stage in the development of human culture." He admits that his fair-minded ideal will nonetheless run into resistance: "Very few scholars in the West will be prepared to admit that any other religion can bear this relation to Christianity." In this light too, he rejects what he sees as the prejudice endemic to Western efforts at comparison, such as presumes "that all other races and cultures have been a preparation for the Greco-Romano-Gothic type, which is now the epitome of Mankind, the representative of Universal Humanity, the heir of all the ages." Such uneven comparisons pit the advanced (Christian) vs the primitive (Asian). He readily criticizes such ventures as giving a bad name to comparison, though he is quite aware that "the hardy 'oriental' who would presume to question this almost axiomatic truth is likely to provoke 'amused' incredulity, if not unmixed derision."

But Seal does more than denounce prejudice that pretends to be "axiomatic truth." He seeks to dig deeper so as to expose the underlying, "essentially wrong conception of the philosophy of history and the evolution of culture," and the "essentially perverse use of the historico-comparative method."[28] Constructively, he proposes a method commensurate with the complexities of the religions compared and free of the vice of "an unhistorical and unreal simplicity, a desire to reduce the variety of Life and Nature to a uniform formula." On the contrary, he proposes textual rigor and respect for history within each cultural context, optimistic that with a sound methodology proper comparison between religions is just as possible as in other fields. But this requires sophistication regarding history. A mere appeal to "the spiritual experiences of the race" is unlikely to produce fruitful insights, since "the higher, more advanced, more complex stages in the history of life, civilisation and culture, are altogether inexplicable on this method, and have been quietly ignored or else travestied."[29]

While history has been divisive, acknowledged difficulties need not thwart the recognition of a universal humanity whereupon "to lay the foundation of a true Philosophy of Universal History," such as would be actually more than "mere European side-views of Humanity for the world's panorama."[30] The universal perspective attains to a truth which no tradition owns and which cannot be revealed as exclusive to any one tradition:

> From the statical point of view, Universal Humanity, though present in each race, is diversely embodied, reflected in specific modes and forms. The Ideal of Humanity is not completely unfolded in any, for each race potentially contains the fullness of the ideal, but actually renders a few phases only, some expressing lower or fewer, others higher or more numerous ones.[31]

This is a very good way of putting it: traditions share a wide range of insights and values across the globe; none is in charge of all of them; we need to learn from one another what has been better articulated in traditions other than our own.

But Seal is not a romantic, at least not to the exclusion of the hard work of scholarship. The "universal culture" or "universal history" is accessible only by "the new, corrected, extended Historic Method which, in consonance with the formula of Evolution rightly understood, and in co-operation with the comparative Method properly qualified, will serve as the organon of the human or sociological Sciences." Once the groundwork for improved understanding of all cultures has been done, the universal-historical method facilitates better comparisons, and in a wide range of fields, including religion, art, and philosophy:

> Chinese, Hindoo, Mohammedan culture-histories, therefore, require to be worked out on the same general historic plan, and in obedience to the same general law of progress, as European civilisation has been, in the different departments of Economy, Social Institutions, Jurisprudence, Politics, Religion, Art and Philosophy.

As a result, there will be "new and comprehensive material for accurate generalisations, for the discovery of general laws of the social organism, alike statical and dynamical."[32]

Reversing the conventional Western wisdom of his times (though in a way consonant with Westcott's hope that Indian Christianity will rejuvenate Christianity in the West), Seal believes that this new comparative work will reinvigorate Europe, now "afflicted with the curse of barrenness." In Europe, "there is a great deal of criticism, and of true and luminous criticism, in religion and in philosophy, but no creation." The West has lost a larger vision of "the realm of the Infinite and the Absolute"; a "firm grasp of Universality"; an "overpowering sense of the invisible world of which our spirits are denizens even now and here"; and a "vision of the Divine in the Human, not in remote history but in the living present." At present, the West is suffering a fragmentation of knowledge and is being pulled apart by "the bewildering complexity of phenomenal knowledge and the multitudinous interests of the special sciences."[33] At this point, the Hindu tradition's energy for the universal fills the gap:

> The speculative ardor, the metaphysical genius, the science of the Absolute, of the Hindus, are exactly fitted to infuse a new blood into European philosophy, and to rouse its dormant activity. The Hindu sees the species in the individual, the essence in the appearance, the intelligence in the intelligible, the ideal in the real. Above all, he has a sense of cosmic unity which enables him to see the whole in the part. And connected with this is the Hindu's

> supreme gift of unifying thought and life, speculation and practice, philosophy and religion.[34]

If the Hindu tradition adopts rigorous comparative methods, and if the West recognizes that it has much to learn from the Hindu traditions, the result will be a renaissance that is religious as well as philosophical. Christianity will throw off its imperial garb and learn again to absorb different cultures rather than trying to conquer or deny them. This renewed absorption, practiced in early Christianity, has to do with learning from the other without a destructive digestion of it. In this way Christians will find meeting points with Hinduism:

> The Hindu God-consciousness, for example, in its threefold manifestation of Brahma, Paramatma and Bhagavan, the Hindu ideal of Jivanmukti (Life Everlasting in this earthly life), with its two elements of divine communion, Yoga and Lila, and the Hindu harmony of the essential disciplines of Jnana, Bhakti and Karma (Knowledge, Faith and Works), will be the fundamental points of contact between Christian Gnosis and Faith on the one hand, and the Hindu philosophico-religious consciousness on the other.[35]

As a result, a better and freer Christianity will reemerge, freed of "the husks of outer creed and dogma," and ready to "take its stand on the inner spiritual experiences and verities of life, and the laws of progress and evolution – the unfolding of the successive stages – in the life of the spirit."[36] This, I suggest, is not merely mystical wishful thinking, but a theological mind at work; while Seal's gnostic animosity to creed and dogma seems ill-informed and unnecessary with respect to his larger purposes, the idea that the relation between India and the West requires the retrieval of fundamental intellectual and spiritual values is relevant even today.

By endeavoring to fashion a proper comparative method, Seal seeks also to overthrow a linear, from East to West, Hegelian model of history. Once the complexity of each tradition is recognized, notions of a linear East-to-West evolution, which has been used in the past to exalt the Christian, will be exposed as lacking in credibility. Indeed, it is already the case that

> with the ethnological material at our disposal, it is a gross and stupid blunder to link Chinese, Hindu, Semitic, Greek, Roman, Gothic, Teutonic cultures, in one line of filiation, in one logical (if not chronological) series. At the present stage of sociological

> research, this amounts to ignorant quackery, a true anachronism, and is totally unworthy of any man of scientific pretensions. No race or civilisation with a continuous history represents a single point or moment.[37]

There is much here of general interest, even in the first few pages of Seal's study. Unfortunately, we cannot go deeper in this lecture into the entirety of his treatise. It is important to note, however, that in the bulk of it Seal practices what he preaches. He aims at the historical sophistication he claims is necessary, in order to show how the myth of Narada's Pilgrimage to Svetadvipa is in certain ways indebted to Christian sources. Proper historical research confirms this connection between Vaisnava and Christian traditions, founded on the commonality of the traditions in regard to their place in the "development of the absolute ideal." In the end, we have an interesting mix of the historical, the comparative, and a certain kind of theology:

> Judged by these two primary factors, in other words, from a historico-comparative survey of the Vaishnava and the Christian idea of the Godhead (symbolized in their Trinities), and the Vaishnava and the Christian view of man's relation to the world and society, these two religions, in spite of marked racial differences, belong to the same stadium in the development of the absolute Idea, and the unfolding plan of Universal History.[38]

The larger purpose of Seal's diligent study of the Narada "pilgrimage," recounted in the Narayaniya section of the Mahabharata, is

> to show by an application of the comparative method hedged round with these qualifications and restrictions that all the conditions of moral certainty are satisfied in this case, in favour of an Eastern Christian influence – (especially of the Gnostic and Syrian cults) in the early centuries of the Christian era, on the development of a particular branch of the Vaishnava creed.[39]

He expects

> a minute exegesis and textual examination of the Mahabharata record in question, and of Nilkantha's commentary, with a view to determine the exact nature and weight of the evidence, if any, in favour of a journey or voyage to Syria or some neighbouring centre of Christianity.

The treatment of the pilgrimage itself takes up most of pages 30–90 of this text of just over one hundred pages, the rest being occupied with Seal's reflection first on related Hindu texts,[40] and then on early Christian parallels. Much of the work may be said simply to demonstrate how to do the study of traditions, and then comparison of traditions, properly; more specifically, he is arguing for the distinct and coherent development of Christian and Vaisnava traditions, but also for clear cases of interdependence and borrowing. Noticing these borrowings, without making too much of them, is in Seal's view necessary for a mature sense of the particular and universal history of the human race and its religions and philosophies. Near the end of his treatise, Seal asserts that

> the evidence I have put forward appears to me to be of such a startling character that I believe it will be considered to be decisive of an actual historical contact between the two cults in the fourth or fifth century of the Christian era.

This real, albeit small, contact is to be placed in the context of a more sophisticated appreciation of both traditions. On the one hand, "Vaishnavism has developed on lines of its own, viz., on the basis of a half-philosophical half-mythological synthesis of the Sankhya and Vedanta systems," while on the other, "Christianity in the West very early forsook Platonism, Neo-platonism and Gnosticism – the counterpart of the Indian Sankhya-cum-Vedanta cult, and received its philosophical mould from the metaphysical and ontological scheme of Aristotle as understood by the Schoolmen and the Arabian philosophers."[41]

For Seal, the divergences and choices made are as illuminating as the moments of mutual indebtedness. In the end, the contact with Christianity had a good effect on Vaishavism, yet without indicating that the latter is derivative of the former:

> I have also shown that the Christian experiences of the Indian Vaishnavas served to liberalise and universalise their faith, and perhaps also to impart a character of jealous, if not militant, unitarianism (*ekantibhava*) to the cult of Krishna-worship. … But, at the same time, the history of doctrine, general as well as particular, must have shown that not a single dogma or rite was derived by the Indian Vaishnava from primitive Christianity.[42]

The fact of relationships and of mutual exchange proves nothing about the essence of these traditions, even if, by the theory of "race-history" adopted by Seal, they represent "with more or less of specific and racial differences, the same stadium in the development of the Absolute Idea, or the history of universal culture."[43]

On the whole, Seal's *Comparative Studies* is a remarkably thoughtful instance of comparison, sophisticated and cognizant of pitfalls, that too is open to both philosophical and theological concerns; and it was undertaken from a consciously Indian and Hindu perspective. It stands out for the rigor of its method, its depth of detail, and its sober insistence on separating out matters of dependence and derivation from simpler patterns of resemblance. Moreover, even if the details of Seal's research require updating more than a hundred years later, his model is pertinent to our quest to diagnose the challenges that have faced and will face Hindu–Christian studies: the need for detailed study; resistance to meta-narratives that relegate Hindu intellectual views to details for study; and, yet, in the end, the insistence on the possibility of comprehensive, universal claims. What do we have in common that is significant, worth sharing in the particular, and without any rush to overarching theories that explain away the detail and put an end to the learning?

Although neither Govindacharya nor Seal offers an exact model for our way forward today, I have spent a number of pages considering them because they are early examples of sustained work in Hindu–Christian studies undertaken from a Hindu perspective. They see the difficulties, do the work, and hold forth some hope that mutual understanding might occur. Both Govindacharya's search for a third space amicable to both Hindus and Christians, and Seal's insistence on context and history as the ground for better religious comparisons, support my intuition that Hindu–Christian studies can advance as an intellectually and spiritually viable field of study.

Some key Hindu intellectuals in mid-century

I continue my inquiry into the 20th-century Hindu intellectual engagement with the Christian West by an equally brief consideration of five key intellectuals: Krishna Chandra Bhattacharyya, Sarvepalli Radhakrishnan, Bimal Krishna Matilal, Kotta Satchidananda Murty, and Daya Krishna. These too are scholars who have seriously and responsibly engaged Western and Christian thinking, showing us their own versions of Hindu–Christian studies in action. (I also have occasion to consider Robert C. Zaehner, who held the Spalding Chair at the University of Oxford between Radhakrishnan and Matilal.)

Krishna Chandra Bhattacaryya

Krishna Chandra Bhattacharyya (1875–1949) was one of the leading Indian philosophers of the first half of the 20th century, and author of a number of noteworthy philosophical studies. But it is in a small essay, "Swaraj in Ideas" (1929), that we see some of his core principles at work. In it, he urges his readers to aim for a true and honorable synthesis of East and West, deeply intellectual, and not driven by extraneous considerations. In this lecture, intended for a group of students, Bhattacharyya elegantly and with deep insight highlights the problem of the contemporary (then, yet still relevant today) Indian intellectual. At the start, he acknowledges the political upheaval of his time and the stains of colonial rule, and then aims at exposing rather "a subtler domination exercised in the sphere of ideas by one culture on another, a domination all the more serious in the consequence, because it is not ordinarily felt."[44] Indian ways of thinking had been superseded and ignored, almost without anyone noticing or anyone caring. Indian intellectuals ended up, all too often, representing and channeling European modes of thinking. In this context, comparison of ideas is hardly possible:

> Under the present system we generally receive western culture in the first instance and then we sometimes try to peer into our ancient culture as a curiosity and with the attitude of foreign oriental scholars and yet we say that this ancient culture of ours is no curiosity.

As a result, "many of our educated men do not know and do not care to know this indigenous nature of ours,"[45] and there has been little rethinking of the West in Indian terms. Bhattacharyya laments that

> in philosophy hardly anything that has been written by a modern educated Indian shows that he has achieved a synthesis of Indian thought with western thought. There is nothing like a judgment on western systems from the standpoint of Indian philosophy, and although some appraisement of Indian philosophy has been attempted from the western standpoint, there appears to be no recognition yet that a criticism of the fundamental notions of either philosophy is necessary before there can be any useful comparative estimate.

Mutual learning is obviously unlikely under these conditions. This is all the more lamentable, since "the most prominent contribution of ancient India to the culture of the world is in the field of Philosophy," and "it is in philosophy that one could look for an effective contact between Eastern and Western ideas." The challenge to philosophers is formidable, since philosophy "has to confront Eastern thought and Western thought with one another and attempt a synthesis or a reasoned rejection of either, if that were possible." Even more ambitiously,

> it is in philosophy, if anywhere, that the task of discovering the soul of India is imperative for the modern India. … Genius can unveil the soul of India in art but it is through philosophy that we can methodically attempt to discover it.[46]

In the engagement of East and West, some adjustments are to be expected, and "we have to accept facts and adapt our secular life and secular ideas to the times." In the spiritual realm, however, ideals cannot be compromised merely "in order to have a smooth sailing with the times"; rather, "if possible and so far as lies in our power, the times have to be adapted to our life and not our life to the times."[47] Intellectual resistance is appropriate, along with some discriminating choices as to where adaptation is appropriate or not:

> The ideals of a community spring from its past history and from the soil: they have not necessarily a universal application, and they are not always self-luminous to other communities. There are ideals of the West which we may respect from a distance without recognizing any specific appeal to ourselves. Then again there are ideals that have a partial appeal to us, because they have an affinity with our own ideals, though still with a foreign complexion.

Here, Indian intellectuals need to decide what kind of appropriation is desirable: "The form of practical life in which an ideal has to be translated, has to be decided by ourselves according to the genius of our own community," and in accord with Indian dignity. Granting that accommodation is demanded, "the foreign ideal is to be assimilated to our ideal and not the other way. There is no demand for the surrender of our individuality in any case."[48]

With all these warnings and cautions in place, Bhattacharyya still speaks on behalf of inclusive learning: "There is, however, a case for universalism. The progress of a community and of humanity implies a gradual simplification and unification of ideals," in accord with a shared power to reason. For this vision to come true in a proper fashion, however, one must eschew reductive reasoning that produces a "simplification and generalization of ideals" due to its "unregenerate understanding with its mechanical separation of the essential from the inessential." Such distillations are based on whim,

> through the accidental likes and dislikes of the person judging. Customs and institutions bound up with age-long sentiments are brushed aside (in the name of reason) as meaningless and dead without any imaginative effort to realize them in an attitude of humility.

If traditions are simply discarded in eagerness for the universal, the cost is the loss of the required reverence and "deepened spiritual insight."

Rather, the required reasoning is born "after the travail of the spirit: rationalism is here the efflux of reverence, reverence for the traditional institutions through which customary sentiments are deepened into transparent ideals." At the same time, change is inevitable, and sentimental clinging to old ideas not justified: "It is well to recognize the need of humility and patience in the adjustment of the world of ideas. Order is evolved in the world of our ideas through infinite patience and humility. That is the right kind of rationalism."[49] Bhattacharyya's rich form of humane critical thinking is rather distant from the detached, analytic version of modern philosophy, and more akin to a theology that is integrally and fully imagined. The balance he seeks and the dangers he envisions do much to clarify and enhance the frame within which the field of Hindu–Christian studies can flourish.

Sarvepalli Radhakrishnan

I wish now to consider together, for a focused moment of comparative insight, the first three Spalding Professors of Eastern Religion and Ethics: Sarvepalli Radhakrishnan (1888–1975), Robert C. Zaehner (1913–1974), and Bimal Krishna Matilal (1935–1991).

Radhakrishnan, the famed scholar of Indian philosophy and respected statesman, merits serious attention in East–West cultural and philosophical exchange, and likewise in the exchange that is or can be Hindu–Christian studies. He has been studied at length, of course, and this lecture is not the place to attempt to expand the scholarship about him. But some useful comments can be made. It is not surprising to note that he was interested in creating a space for Indian intellectual work, and was one of the leading, internationally known intellectuals in the mid-20th century. Today most scholars would look to his writing not for the latest Indological insights, but to observe a leading Indian intellectual engaging Western thought, so as to make space for his traditions. We can see this compactly in "The World's Unborn Soul" (1936), his inaugural lecture at Oxford as the first Spalding professor.[50]

More than half the lecture assesses the long efforts in the West, among Jews and Greeks, Christians and modern secularists, to find a proper way of understanding God and religion, so as to be faithful to tradition while yet also rebuilding the foundations for a viable rational – and then academic – ground for the ensuing intellectual work. At various points in history, these Western intellectuals have become curious about cultures other than their own, and gone to great lengths to study the religious other. The inevitable interaction of cultures is on the whole a good thing, since "the great periods of human history are marked by a widespread access of spiritual vitality derived from the fusion of national cultures with foreign influences," as history shows; even "the transition to the modern world was marked by the recovery of the Ancient." Eras of uncertainty and great internal change are not times to close off the outsider, since "in times of trouble we draw the profoundest inspiration from sources outside us, from the newly recovered past or the achievement of men under different skies." Accordingly, Radhakrishnan tells his Oxford audience, "the civilizations of the East, their religions and ethics, may offer us some help in negotiating difficulties that we are up against."[51] The underlying point is clear: the West needs to do more than retrieve its own premodern traditions, and must recognize that "there are others also who have participated in the supreme adventure of the ages, the prophets of Egypt, the sages of China, and the seers of India, who are guide-posts disclosing to us the course of the trail."[52]

Radhakrishnan praises the Spalding family for countering the notion that Hindu thought has no relevance to the West, and for their "desire to lift Eastern thought from its sheltered remoteness and indicate its enduring value as a living force in shaping the soul of the modern man."[53] They are right, since Hinduism, in contrast with the West (but like Buddhism), stresses experience as a source of true knowledge. With a certain aggressiveness, he asserts that experience is an epistemologically relevant category: "To say that God exists means that spiritual experience is attainable. The possibility of the experience constitutes the most conclusive proof of the reality of God." God is "the factual content of the spiritual experience." Intending to provoke, I think, he adds that

> all other proofs are descriptions of God, matters of definition, and language … the fact of God does not depend on mere human

> authority or evidence from alleged miraculous events. The authority of scripture, the traditions of the Church, or the casuistries of schoolmen who proclaim but do not prove, may not carry conviction to many of us who are the children of science and reason.

By contrast,

> we must submit to the fact of spiritual experience, which is primary and positive. We may dispute theologies, but cannot deny facts. The fire of life in its visible burning compels assent, though not the fumbling speculations of smokers sitting around the fire.[54]

Even though he puts experience in the center, as relevant to the study of religions at Oxford, Radhakrishnan does not get personal about his own experience. By contrast, those who deny the importance of experience are those "who have no contact with reality, no insight into truth," rather substituting "the relative symbol for the absolute truth." They are clever, but "in their self-confident jugglery with symbols and definitions they forget the thing itself." Without a grounding in experience, words are empty, not "significant expressions of truth."[55]

He ends on a hopeful note: if we put aside the narrow interests of "a powerful privileged few" individuals and nations, we come to realize

> the gradual dawning of a great light, a converging life endeavour, a growing realization that there is a secret spirit in which we are all one, and of which humanity is the highest vehicle on earth, and an increasing desire to live out this knowledge and establish a kingdom of spirit on earth.[56]

Even in a university setting,

> the obstacles of religious dogma are not so formidable as they were in the past. The progress of thought and criticism is helping the different religions to sound the note of the eternal, the universal, the one truth of spirit which life obeys, seeks for, and delights in at all times and in all places.

The truth of a religion is not (merely) what is singular or different, nor its norms and rules, but rather "that part of it which it is capable of sharing with all others."[57]

The inaugural lecture is printed as the first essay in the collection known as *Eastern Religions and Western Thought*. The eighth essay in that same volume, "Meeting of Religions," extends Radhakrishnan's vision. Here he narrates the history of Hinduism, compared and contrasted with the other religions of the world, and here too he is impatient with religions which do not yet have an open, inclusive view of the world. The future is in the hands of liberals who put aside doctrinaire exclusions, and instead envision the religious of the world as all working together:

> In their wide environment, religions are assisting each other to find their own souls and grow to their full stature. Owing to a cross-fertilization of ideas and insights, behind which lie centuries of racial and cultural tradition; and earnest endeavour, a great unification is taking place in the deeper fabric of men's thoughts. … We are slowly realizing that believers with different opinions and convictions are necessary to each other to work out the larger synthesis which alone can give the spiritual basis to a world brought together into intimate oneness by man's mechanical ingenuity.[58]

This is a plausible way forward, provided there is a sufficient number of religious intellectuals with the energy to dig deep in their own traditions, while also having the spiritual and intellectual sensitivities requisite for learning across religious borders; and such too is the work of a constructive Hindu–Christian studies.

A note on Robert C. Zaehner's rejoinder

The second Spalding Professor was Robert C. Zaehner (1913–1974). This British Christian was not by training a scholar of Hinduism nor, at least at the time of his lecture, was he hopeful regarding the possibility of interreligious studies having any value in a university setting. In "Foolishness to the Greeks" (1953), he expressed his own skepticism about East–West possibilities. Zaehner barely refers to Radhakrishnan, and the spirit of his lecture is far removed from both Radhakrishnan's open view of the project of the chair and, at least in the short run, the Spalding ideal itself. At the beginning of the lecture, he duly notes the purposes of the chair:

> The Professorship would seem to have three main functions: i. to build up in this University a permanent interest in the great religious systems of the world, by which are commonly understood Confucianism, Taoism, Hinduism, Buddhism, Zoroastrianism,

> Judaism, Islam, and Christianity; ii. to interpret, compare, and contrast these systems; and iii. to bring them together in closer understanding, harmony, and friendship.[59]

In a blunt manner that will surely have displeased his audience he then narrows greatly what he thinks can be done at a university:

> Of these functions only the first and second would normally fall within the scope of an academic discipline. The third – the promotion of understanding between the great religions – can hardly be pursued in a British university where the non-Christian religions can scarcely be said to be represented at all.[60]

Indeed, Zaehner does not think that

> it can be a legitimate function of a university professor to attempt to induce harmony among elements as disparate as the great religions of mankind appear to be, if, as seems inevitable, the resultant harmony is only to be apparent, verbal, and therefore fictitious. Such a procedure may well be commendable in a statesman. In a profession that concerns itself with the pursuit of truth it is damnable.[61]

But why are the non-Christian religions missing at Oxford? For Zaehner, three features of the modern Western university militate against such learning and, by extension I suggest, against interreligious learning. First, there is "the progressive secularization of the University." Second, "the Christian minority" is close-minded, seeming not only "to take it for granted that God has revealed Himself once and for all through, Jesus Christ," but by this attitude then "to ignore the other world religions completely or to treat them with a tolerant contempt." Third, "the spread of secularist ideas throughout the educated classes of the Orient" is undermining "societies hitherto firmly based on a given religion," a move that in turn aggravates "the fear of the more conservative-minded that the comparative study of religions can only lead to a further loss of faith in the traditional creeds, since these creeds are so manifestly at loggerheads with one another."[62] In the end, "there is a very real danger that an exclusively rationalist outlook will put a further barrier between ourselves and the Eastern countries still associated with us."

The future too is dim, says Zaehner. If reason dominates, it may lead to the abandonment of doctrine; if reason is cast aside, a-rational dogmatisms will simply clash with one another.[63] Even actual comparative work undermines the hoped-for mutual learning, for it shows us that we have less in common than imagined. This is because the "basic principles of Eastern and Western – which in practice means Indian and Semitic – are, I will not say irreconcilably opposed; they are simply not starting from the same premisses."[64] Beyond a general affirmation of the value of release from this world, it turns out that there is no agreement on what release means or how it is to be achieved. It therefore makes no sense "to discuss either Hinduism or Buddhism in Christian terms," and "it is at least as foolish to try to bring the New Testament into harmony with the Vedanta," since they "do not deal with the same subject-matter."[65] It is clear then that at this point in his career, Zaehner could be counted among those skeptical about the very idea of a constructive Hindu–Christian exchange that is intellectual, spiritual, and still properly academic. Even if his own thinking evolved later on, the skepticism manifest in his lecture is still alive today, a force eroding the desire for and confidence in the possibility of Hindu–Christian studies. But Zaehner's was not the last word, and his skepticism did not indicate a consensus on turning away from the project of interreligious learning.

Bimal Krishna Matilal

Bimal Krishna Matilal (1935–1991) was the third holder of the chair. He was a distinguished scholar who had studied at Harvard and taught at the University of Chicago and other prestigious universities. "The Logical Illumination of Indian Mysticism" is his inaugural Spalding lecture, delivered in 1977. The lecture is marked by a gentlemanly courtesy toward his predecessor, even as he distances himself from Zaehner on several points. In what is probably a nod to Radhakrishnan and a mild critique of Zaehner, he observes,

> Both the religious man and the rational man in our society today raise their eyebrows at the question of "rational comprehension" of the religious and the mystical. For the rational man believes that religion is basically irrational; it is, at its best, above and beyond reason, and, at its worst, is below reason. The religious man will hesitate because, for him, religion is based on experience or on faith or on both. Hence, he would argue, it is impossible for an agnostic, who lacks any experience, either religious or mystical, to have a rational comprehension of religion or mysticism.[66]

Perhaps playing the peacemaker, Matilal cautions against a merely rational assessment of religion:

> Man is a rational animal, but, what is more interesting, he is not exclusively rational. Hence, he continues to search for the "promised" land, for the "sacred", for nirvana. It has been claimed by the sociologist that human civilization is but a fabrication of a child afraid to be alone in the dark. And religion is part of that civilization. Man also has a monkey inside him, which prompts him to ask rational questions and demand rational answers. Otherwise, we would not have a Socrates, or an Aristotle, or a Buddha, or a Nagarjuna, or a Sriharsa.

Indeed, reason itself then turns out to be more religiously potent than imagined: "As my predecessor [Zaehner] used often to say, quoting a phrase of Al-Ghazali, 'for reason is God's scale on earth'."[67] If we are mindful of the deep humanity of being-religious, our study itself creates possibilities for true interreligious learning.

Two related essays of Matilal bear mention. First, the brief "Indian Philosophy: Is There a Problem Today?" marks off a number of possible meanings of "Indian philosophy." It can be a term used in comparison and contrast with "Greek philosophy," "Chinese philosophy," etc., and more as "a philological exercise than a philosophical discipline."[68] It can mark off an area of historical study, within a general history of philosophy. "Indian philosophy" may be depicted, ambivalently, as more spiritual, other-worldly, or more robustly intellectual *and* moksa-oriented. Or it can refer to rigorous thinking "buried under the treasure-chest of Sanskrit"[69] which, if weakened to *moksa-sastra*, becomes a softer and less compelling version of true knowledge. Or "philosophy" may be used as to describe how some Indian intellectuals are thinking today "vis-à-vis their Western compatriots." But if so, it is fair to ask, "What contributions, if any, have they made recently to the field of 'philosophy' by which one may understand simple Western philosophic tradition?"[70] This opens up a field for comparative study, a field which can justly be defended once properly understood: "'Comparative philosophy' has acquired a bad reputation mainly because of the failures and lack of depth of the early comparativists," who "not only misunderstood the nature and the extent of the problem they were trying to grapple with," but also "lacked insights and adequate preparation" for the rigorous work before them. Properly envisioned, the task of the Indian philosopher is to create an open space where thinking-together can occur:

> The purpose of the Indian philosopher today, who chooses to work on the classical systems, is to interpret and thereby offer a

> medium where philosophers, using the word to mean those who pursue rationally arguable answers to meaningful questions, both Indian and Western, may converse.

This is the creation of an intellectually fertile third space, wherein both classical traditions and modern thinkers can be taken seriously.[71]

In the still briefer "The Problem of Inter-faith Studies,"[72] Matilal notes how Zaehner softened in the years after his Spalding lecture and became more open to attending to both similarities and differences among religions. But then Matilal himself questions the worth of irenic interreligious exchange, asking whether interreligious exchange can be productive; he doubts whether this can be so, since the right intellectual-spiritual balance is elusive:

> The basic principles of great religions of the world, that is, of Eastern and Western religions, are so different from each other that it is practically impossible to move between such worlds. One may, of course, try, so the argument goes, to read the texts and scriptures of another religion, with an academic interest, but he will never be able to "catch its inner spirit" (whatever the phrase means).[73]

But such skepticism depends on two problematic presuppositions: one has to believe in something to understand it; someone without religious experience cannot understand the pertinent religion. Philosophically, the matter may be posed as the problem of the linguist who tries both to learn a new language and translate into it, and realizes that this cannot be done. If we are to "transform two monologues into a dialogue," Matilal insists that we need a willingness to listen and a readiness to seek out "some common thought patterns between the participants." But such patterns do exist in the "great religions of the world."[74] In turn, further dispositions are required: humility in the face of mystery, and the positing of some other, higher reality than the empirical. In the end, the philosopher has an in-between vocation, between the skeptics and the believers: "the philosopher is the one who stays on the borderline and observes both sides."[75] In the religions India and the West can meet, and the philosopher is well suited to stand at the meeting point in that encounter; it seems more natural, though, to speak of this "philosopher" as a religious intellectual, engaged in the richer learning that here we are calling Hindu–Christian studies.

Kotta Satchidananda Murty

I cannot miss the opportunity to name two other important intellectuals of the 20th century, who too are models for the kind of integral thinking through and with the West that I have in mind. Kotta Satchidananda Murty (1924–2011) was a well-known and influential Hindu intellectual whose work has received less attention in the West than it merits. Throughout his long career he was acutely aware of the dynamics of comparative, cross-cultural learning and, most importantly for our purposes, he was a leading practitioner of substantive comparative learning. *Revelation and Reason in Advaita Vedanta* (1959) stands forth as a sophisticated and impressively theological book that explicitly engages the challenges related to Hindu–Christian studies. As such, it shows us a viable (even if of course slightly dated) model for how such studies might best proceed. While the book reviews reason and revelation in Advaita and other classical Indian systems, it is also a constructive work of Hindu reflection, in which Murty's effortless flow back and forth among the views of respected intellectuals East and West is notable. His comparative inquiry is not artificial or forced, since he is ready to learn naturally from whichever sources seem right, in order to make a necessary point. In the book's preface, aware that some readers may want more or less Indology or comparative learning, Murty defends his combination in Part One of so much information on Vedanta and other *darsana*s with so much comparative work with Western theologies in Part Two: depth in the former is required to set up a topic properly, while learning from outside the Hindu traditions sheds new light on ideas and insights in that tradition. In his preface he admits that philosophically he sides with Jayanta Bhatta, and religiously with Ramanuja; such views are not surprising, but he admits them with admirable equanimity. It is notable that his Indian and Hindu roots do not soften his critical edge regarding Indian traditions. He can criticize Advaita, just as he can credibly argue with Barth and Brunner.

The essays collected in *The Realm of Between: Lectures on the Philosophy of Religion* (1973) offer specific and pointed comparisons with Western thought, even as Murty eschews vaguer claims about mystical connections among traditions.[76] For example, "Religious Action" expertly and simply surveys a series of Vedic and Hindu views of sacrifice and the relation of deity to sacrificial action, and shows how Mimamsa effectively and with firm logic forecloses on notions of independent deities. One learns a tradition "by the study and methodical investigation of religious tradition and by thinking over it, … so that the wisdom of the past may be transformed by reflection into principles for guidance of action."[77] In the major portion of the essay, Murty describes the ancient Indian view of sacrifice in some depth and detail. For the sake of clarification, he makes brief comparisons, with "the doctrines of Socrates, Epicurus and Kant in Europe and of Confucius and the Gita in Asia."[78] Longer reflections of the views of Aurobindo and Heidegger show how they turn to symbolic psychology (Aurobindo) or an opening into the unknown and even the realm of dread (Heidegger) in order to elucidate the meaning of sacrifice; Murty thus widens the lens through which the idea and practice of sacrifice might be read.

Murty is a true comparativist, since he crosses cultural, philosophical, and religious boundaries, to show not merely that comparative thinking is possible, but also that it is worthwhile for the sake of authentically thinking through the implications of claims about reason and revelation. Indeed, Murty is more than a Hindu who has studied about Christian and Western thought; he is rather a Hindu-Christian intellectual. Nor is he a comparativist for the sake of comparison, or for the sake of dialogue; he undertakes the work in order to be and remain an Indian and Hindu intellectual. He *thinks* across the boundaries, and does so with notable attention to the religious dimensions of the philosophical issues at hand. He is thus an ideal interlocutor regarding Hindu–Christian studies, as he opens the possibility of cross-cultural and interreligious learning on each subject at hand, a process not thwarted by hesitation, or cultural diffidence, or concern to show the uniqueness of every Hindu idea.

Daya Krishna

Daya Krishna (1924–2007) was editor of the *Journal of the Indian Council of Philosophical Research* for over three decades, and author of many provocative essays that engage the West culturally and philosophically. He effectively problematized the habits and expectations usually brought to the rapprochement of India and the West, and, by my extension, to the ideal and reality of Hindu–Christian studies. In "Comparative Philosophy: What It Is and What It Ought to Be,"[79] for instance, Krishna raises critical questions about the project of comparative philosophy. Such a field will be considered either trivial or impossible, depending on whether philosophizing is truly universal or not. Following Bhattacharyya in this regard, Krishna too criticizes what he finds to be unproductive swings between desires for similarity and for difference:

> The Indian scholars who have concerned themselves with philosophy, for example, not only have swallowed the bait hook, line, and sinker but have tried to gain respectability for Indian philosophy either by discovering parallels to most of the western philosophical positions in the Indian tradition or by taking pride in the fact that philosophy in India was no mere arid intellectual exercise engaged in logic-chopping for its own sake, but concerned with the deepest existential issues of the bondage and liberation of man's innermost being.

As a result, many seem unable to decide whether Indian philosophy possesses just what "western philosophy had to show in terms of the utmost sophistication of epistemological and ontological reflection," or rather also contains some "special, unique characteristic of being spiritual and concerned with *moksa*."[80] Krishna deflates any debate on the matter by arguing that a combination of similarity and difference is the only likely conclusion: "It was conveniently forgotten that if philosophy is an enterprise of the human reason, it is bound to show similarities across cultures to some extent"; this is because philosophy as a human enterprise "is bound to be concerned with what man, in a particular culture, regards as the summum bonum for mankind."[81]

Distortion and oversimplification in comparison are traceable to the unreflective habit of clinging uncritically to one set of normative terms and refusing to consider any other set. There should be a normal back and forth by which each culture sees the others "from its own point of reference" and thus becomes "both the subject and object of comparison, in turn." Too often, Indian intellectuals have so internalized Western categories and standards of intelligibility that "they observe, understand, and compare their own cultures (only) in terms given to them by the West."[82] Disclosure of differences is preferable if "each available conceptual structure thus shows the limitations of the others and suggests an alternative possibility unexplored by them." Fruitful comparisons of this sort draw our attention "to those facts of our experience which have been neglected in other perspectives and to ways of organizing and patterning experience that were not seen by them." But an overly subjective turn too would be dangerous, since it "brings the whole cognitive enterprise perilously close to the artistic one and, if taken to its logical conclusion, would make us give up the truth claim altogether."[83] On the contrary, "concepts can never be simply images or symbols and can hardly ever be simply a matter of feelings and emotions." But even if objectivity is possible and matters, the future "will always be there to show us not only the limitations of our knowledge and the falsity of our claims but also to bring to our notice new horizons, undreamed of before."[84]

If attention is focused on differences, and if we recognize how differences prompt interesting problems, comparison then becomes able to liberate the imagination:

> To search for the distinctive philosophical problems seen as problems or for distinctiveness in the solutions offered to similar problems is not only to see the alien tradition in a new way but to enrich oneself with the awareness of an alternative possibility in thought, a possibility that has already been actualized.

This awareness of alternatives can "free one's conceptual imagination from the unconscious constraints of one's own conceptual tradition." Thus, comparative philosophy, simply as good and productive thinking, can be "a mutual liberator of each philosophical tradition from the limitations imposed upon it by its own past." This is, again, a greatly desired alternative to what Krishna identifies as the current situation, which takes for granted "the imposition of the standards of one dominant culture upon all the others and the evaluation of their philosophical achievements in terms of those alien standards."[85] Like Murty, Krishna wants simply to be a rigorous and yet therefore productive intellectual; for that, comparative work is a requirement. This is solid grounding for the kind of comparative, cross-cultural learning we can ambition today, is it not? A viable Hindu–Christian learning too must avoid a one-sided imposition of the questions and methods of Christian tradition, if the challenges and learning are to be mutual. If Hindu intellectuals engage in Hindu–Christian studies, they are simply insisting on being good intellectuals, and in that way they do us the favor of rescuing the field from the monotony of an entirely Christian hold on new knowledge, or of a resistant skepticism and suspicion that make any religious or interreligious learning impossible.

Two contemporary Hindu intellectuals

To conclude this lecture, I wish briefly to recognize two more recent intellectuals, still writing today, whose work highlights some of the possibilities and challenges evident in the quest for a sense of the reciprocity that must be the real background to any forward movement in Hindu–Christian studies: Arvind Sharma and Anantanand Rambachan. Each exemplifies in his own way the possibilities before Indian and Hindu religious intellectuals in our era: the requisite cross-cultural and interreligious thinking is being done – hence it can be done, obstacles notwithstanding.

Arvind Sharma

Arvind Sharma is a respected senior scholar who, holding a PhD from Harvard University, has for many years taught in the West; he is of course not an Indian intellectual working in the Indian context viewing the West only from afar. Even as he has sought to pursue comparative studies and constructive philosophical work from a Hindu perspective, he has always been mindful of the possibilities and constraints of Western academic learning. In *Religious Studies and Comparative Methodology* (2005), he draws on his own Hindu tradition to craft a way of thinking about comparative study that takes Western modes of comparison into account, but that is not prejudicial to his tradition. As he explains,

> Comparisons can be of two kinds – homonymous and synonymous. Homonymous comparisons are between phenomena, which appear similar but are really different, just as homonyms are words with similar sounds but with different meanings. Synonymous comparisons are between phenomena that appear different but possess similar significance in each tradition, just as synonyms are words that have different sounds but are similar in meaning.

He draws interesting implications for religious studies: "Old comparative religion has been oriented toward making homonymous comparisons, but new comparative religion – at least, the kind I would like to practice – will be oriented toward making synonymous comparisons,"[86] which facilitate a non-prejudicial and reciprocal learning: "Now, when synonymous comparisons are made between two traditions, they often result in what I like to call reciprocal illumination. That is to say, one tradition sheds light on the other."[87]

Sharma offers as examples the divinity of Indian Brahmins and European kings, and the resurrections of Jesus and Milarepa. Regarding the latter: homonymously there are interesting similarities and differences between the two resurrections, but these do not decisively render the comparison either impossible or necessary, nor can one in that way undermine or establish the credibility of either example. Resurrection does not have the same status in the two traditions, and as a result one or the other version of the idea is likely to suffer from the comparison. On the whole, such comparisons turn out to be unsatisfying, hardly worth the effort. But a synonymous comparison of the two resurrections is more promising. "The central fact corresponding to resurrection in Christianity is enlightenment in Buddhism … the 'person' of Jesus stands in same relation to the former as the teaching of the Buddha does to the latter."[88] If so, a fairer and more constructive comparison of the Buddhist and Christian realities is possible:

> Thus if it is true, as is being contended, that in Christianity the person of Jesus saves and in Buddhism the teaching of Buddha performs the same role, then doubts about the resurrection of Jesus should be compared to the doubts about Buddha's enlightenment.[89]

Sharma is in certain ways like Brajendranath Seal, aiming to construct an intelligent, workable model of comparison that is fair to both traditions and thus cannot be discounted or ignored by skeptics who would deny the value of comparison on political grounds.

Chapter 9 notes further examples of reciprocal illumination: the practice of suttee, the caste system, the practice of untouchability, and trial by ordeal. In all of these examples, the attitude and enactment of reciprocal illumination shaped contexts in which "my understanding of Hinduism was, if not enriched, enhanced, or enlarged, at least affected and influenced by what I learned of Christianity."[90] In his concluding chapter, Sharma remarks,

> The present study is a prolonged answer to the short question: what if one compares things not in order to judge one item in terms of another, but to see how our understanding of the items themselves is enhanced in the process, or even in some other dimension of religious life that one did not have in mind to begin with. This approach to comparison, which I have called reciprocal illumination, is what this book is all about.[91]

It seems an easy step from reciprocal illumination, as a philosophical venture, to the work of comparative theology, both being supports for Hindu–Christian studies.

Sharma knows very well the current suspicions about comparison and forms of dialogue that rely on the fruitfulness of dialogue, but insists that his reciprocal illumination model avoids much of the criticism:

> The concept of reciprocal illumination as canvassed in the present book is based on a concept of the "end" of comparison rather

> different in its aim. One aim of comparison, according to [Jonathan Z.] Smith, is a "redescription of the exempla (each in the light of the other)" [followed by] "a rectification of the academic categories in relation to which they have been imagined."[92]

Sharma distinguishes his model from Smith's: "In reciprocal illumination no such redescription is involved; only a deeper understanding is achieved." Or, even when redescription is involved, the "illumination of either exemplum may suffice; that of both (prescribed by Smith) is welcome but not required. Similarly, while the rectification of the academic category in the light of the exercise may be desirable, this is not the end sought by reciprocal illumination.".[93]

He defends the seeming non-rigor of his method, admitting that "the ease with which reciprocal illumination can be applied in a given context might create the impression that the concept must lack clarity if it produces such a potpourri of results going in so many directions." But, he insists that "it is the clarity of the central idea [reciprocal illumination] rather than its ambiguity that accounts for the versatility of its applicability." Reciprocal illumination simply "seeks to see how one datum may shed light on another, or two data on each other, rather than on a common or transcendent category, and further seeks to show that apparently different phenomena may also unexpectedly shed similar light."[94] It is a method that fosters mutual exchange across religious borders in a shared space that is dominated by neither Hindus nor Christians. In this way it is akin to comparative theology, which I will discuss in the Epilogue, and one of the resources that makes Hindu–Christian dialogue possibly fruitful and nearly inevitable, simply due to its good intellectual grounds.

Anantanand Rambachan

Anantanand Rambachan is a contemporary Hindu theologian, a highly respected academic, and for nearly thirty years has been a professor at St. Olaf College in Minnesota. Like Sharma, his work is deeply informed by the disciplinary values of the modern academy. I include him here because he consciously draws on contemporary styles of Christian theological writing for substantive Hindu theological writing. He manifests a positive attitude to interreligious learning that has solid intellectual grounds not likely to be unsettled by merely political considerations. His *Hindu Theology of Liberation* exhibits a serenity and confidence quite remarkable in the fraught world of Hindu–Christian studies. For he is, first of all, a Hindu theologian who accepts the idea of "theology" in a thoughtful manner, but also draws primarily on Hindu sources to think through and explain an Advaita view of this world, and the issues facing it today. Rambachan's book consciously models responsibilities and virtues characteristic of a modern Hindu theological text, and is deeply comparative at the same time.

It is also refreshing to note that Rambachan is not concerned primarily with the notion of comparison or with the idea of Hindu–Christian learning. Rather, he crosses such boundaries naturally, as it were, because he wants to address a range of vexed issues that can hardly be contained within any single tradition: patriarchy, homophobia, anthropocentrism, the mistreatment of fetuses and children, and caste. In each case, he argues for a responsible Hindu attitude toward problems that concern all, and not just Christians or Hindus or any particular religious group. The result is a series of fresh insights into issues that too often have been discussed only in terms of Christian and Western views, or by mere appeals to Hindu values uncritically received. His work across the Hindu and Christian borders is not for the sake of promoting or illustrating dialogue – even if he favors it – but rather to use all available resources to confront issues he wanted to confront within his own community.

Prospects for vital Hindu theological engagement with the West

What do all the examples I have offered add up to? I do not wish to argue that the Hindu study of Western thought offers a perfect and timely model for Hindu–Christian studies, any more than I would have been willing to argue for the Jesuit model of learning, as if that were perfect and timely. To conclude this lecture and prepare the way for the next, let us step back for a moment.

In 2001, Parimal Patil, until recently chair of the Department of South Asian Studies at Harvard, at my invitation wrote an afterword, "A Hindu Theologian's Response: A Prolegomenon to 'Christian God, Hindu God,'" that was included in my book *Hindu God, Christian God*. I will refer to several key passages from his response. Pointing to the asymmetry between resources and supports available to Christian and Hindu scholars, Patil emphasizes the agency of Hindu intellectuals, their choices regarding topics and methods:

> Whether theology as interpreted and practiced by the intellectuals to whom Clooney refers is to be a part of Hinduism's future is for Hindus to decide. Whether the intellectual concerns described by

> Clooney will be shared in the future will also depend on whether Hindus and Christians continue to recognize their importance.

Much rectification is required, says Patil, if "theology" is to be more than Christian theology, and Hindu–Christian studies more than Christian intellectual work and, worse still, largely a matter of Christians talking to other Christians. Much practical work has to be done first:

> Without institutional space for Hindu theologians and the study of Hindu theology, moreover, it is difficult to imagine that Hindu traditions would not be more easily misused. Theology must, therefore, either accept its interreligious dimensions through sustained engagement with the voices and texts of others who share this intellectual (and not yet institutional) space or provide principled reasons why this space must be redescribed to exclude, for example, the intellectuals to whom Clooney refers.

Though not entirely unsympathetic to my proposal, Patil was, in 2001 at least, not hopeful about the possibility of the realization of a new, equal interreligious learning in the modern context.[95] The academy militates against the desired exchange, since in such disciplinary contexts,

> constructive and normative work is rarely respected and, in fact, is generally believed to reveal that those who produce it lack the 'scholarly' distance that is necessary for rigorous and responsible work in these disciplines. The participation of Hindu intellectuals in the project described in this work may come, therefore, at a very high professional price.[96]

And even if Hindu religious intellectuals want to do what I was suggesting in my 2001 book, it is still a great challenge, Patil says,

> to maintain the integrity of tradition while attempting to recontextualize it in a context that is, in many ways, intellectually familiar but institutionally new. It is the challenge of forming tradition while continuing to be genuinely formed by it. Such work must have an authentic voice from Hindu tradition and also be a part of the discipline of theology; it must be the work of a Hindu scholar who is also a theologian; and it must serve both the interests of tradition and the needs of the discipline.[97]

This is very hard work indeed; but it is not impossible, even if Patil himself has not followed up on the ways forward that he highlights. It is still very difficult for Indians and Hindus to engage in a fully engaged study of Western or Christian thought, in light of the relative mismatch that still exists between Western academic thought and Hindu thought, with all the personal and economic factors involved. While the relationship is no longer polemical in the way it had been in past eras, entangled in efforts to convert, it is nevertheless clear that, currently, a very large gap remains between a Hindu intellectual community, largely but not only in India, struggling to find the right balance between faith and reason, and a Western array of modes of study, some of which are still very Christian at least in form, and some of which distance themselves entirely from any dynamic of faith and reason, preferring only historical critique and modernist or postmodernist deconstructions of faith, worship, and doctrine. Finding a "third space" between traditions remains difficult, with India's intellectuals still at odds regarding their own tradition, or traditions in their many strands, with the focus shifting between starkly logical and analytic thinking on the one hand, and esoteric perennial and theosophical thinking on the other. And still, unjustly, much of the modern Indian philosophical tradition (whether implicitly theological or not) has been unduly ignored in the West. And so we must admit the limits that constrain the Hindu study of Christianity, even as we can be genuinely hopeful in light of the history of substantive intellectual encounters, as described in this lecture and, with respect to the Christian learning of Hinduism, in the first lecture.

In this light, I note Rajiv Malhotra's *The Battle for Sanskrit: Is Sanskrit Political or Sacred? Oppressive or Liberating? Dead or Alive?* (2016). While Malhotra's polemical tone and predilection for *ad hominem* attacks diminish the book's impact, it has the merit of bringing important issues to the fore, and posing, from inside Hindu tradition, some fair questions to South Asianists and Indologists. The kind of public debate – perhaps literally on a stage, in a theater – that Malhotra seems to envision will not by itself yield the desired understanding. But the goals he states at the book's end are worthy of further attention: (1) the Sanskrit ecosystem must be revived in a holistic way; (2) non-translatable Sanskrit terms must enter the mainstream; (3) *sastra*s must be seen as a platform for innovation; (4) new *itihasa*s and *smrti*s must be written; (5) "sacred philology" must compete against political/liberation philology; (6) the *purva-paksa* tradition must be revived; and (7) well-qualified home teams and institutions must be developed.[98] These points seem to me all worthy of further discussion and, more importantly, work toward implementation. The fact that scholars can readily and fairly raise further questions about much of what Malhotra says ought not to mean that the basic agenda be infinitely postponed or his insights erased. Malhotra's concluding chapter admits "the hard work that is needed," and lists a further set of more specific tasks, such as "contesting the intellectual re-colonization of India."[99] In the context of my lectures, his final comments are apt, including the admission that more study of Christianity is required: "Hinduism would indeed benefit if some of its bright young scholars studied Western thought," even if "few are strong enough to go through this kind of intense study without irrevocably drifting away from Indian thought."[100] Even if it remains impossible to define "Hindu thought" or "Indian thought" definitively, Malhotra's point is well taken, since contemporary methods of study do not mesh well with traditional learning. In a proposal that merits consideration, Malhotra suggests that "the best way to pursue such deep immersion in purva-paksa with the West is in the environment of dharmic commitment, guru guidance and regular sadhana, just as our elders always insisted."[101] This is particularly the case if we seek to avoid merely transplanting problems arising in the Indian context to the context of the West, where missionary proselytization is frowned on from many perspectives. Perhaps it is unexpectedly in the West that new insights and a fresh beginning for Hindu–Christian studies are to be found, in certain strands of the study of religion and religions today.

In its simplest form, my point is to argue that the Hindu study of Western and Christian thought has a long and robust history, and has very often been motivated by spiritual and intellectual concerns arising from within the Hindu context itself. As I have shown, there are older and contemporary examples of substantive intellectual/spiritual Hindu engagement with the West, examples not driven by polite responses to Christian invitations to dialogue, but by another set of necessities – social and political, cultural and religious – that impel a response to the West. It is not true, clearly, that Hindus have never found reason to learn from the West or take the West into account intellectually, as if Hindu–Christian studies is only and merely something Christians do. Despite the uneven ground, and despite Western aggression against Indian culture and religion, real and important learning has occurred, substantively and fruitfully. Certainly, there have also been enormous accommodations of the West, linguistically by writing in English, and categorically by thinking in accord with Western concepts. But there has also been significant effort to create new categories that better serve the comparative project, instead of thwarting from the start the prospects for a true Indian contribution to the hoped-for learning. There is much to be hopeful for here, once we start paying attention to the quieter scholarship that has flourished outside the glare of missionary and political engagements.

But my optimism should not be taken to suggest that the thinkers considered in this lecture offer a simple and straightforward model for Hindu–Christian studies today, any more than did the Jesuit missionary scholars. Much of what we have seen is indeed relevant, but more work needs to be done to ensure that this learning attains the integral spiritual and intellectual encounter with Christian tradition that is required. Needed still is a more articulate version of religious intellectual inquiry that also includes the theological, grounded in persons, their experience, and communal perspectives. I wish now to suggest that this fuller relevant learning can be mediated through some of the best practices arising in the modern study of religions in modern academe, even if that academic study has often vexed both Hindus and Christians. My third lecture will propose ways in which we are to learn from certain strands of modern academic study.

Notes

1 Ruparell 2000: 26.
2 See also Clooney 2004 and Klostermeier 2011.
3 All three lectures were given on February 17, 1897.
4 Govindacharya 1897: 7.
5 Ibid.
6 Ibid.
7 Earlier, Govindacharya praises Proclus and the Alexandrian School for the unification of philosophy and theology but laments the collapse of that synthesis among the early Christian fathers: "The divorce of Faith from Philosophy has been the ruin of Christianity" (ibid., 46)
8 Citations are from lecture 1, 67–68. Even more specifically he adds, "If like Father Rickaby in his treatise on Moral Philosophy in the Stonyhurst Series of Manuals of Catholic Philosophy, the definition of soul be given as including the 'appetites' of man, the view presents itself to the Vedantist as at once grotesque" (ibid., 68).
9 Ibid.
10 Ibid., 71.
11 Ibid., 33.
12 Ibid., 32.
13 Ibid, 33.
14 Ibid, 54–57.
15 Ibid., 78.
16 Ibid., 79.
17 Ibid., 82–83.
18 Ibid., 7.

19 Ibid., 3.
20 Ibid., 11, citing Vivekananda, the *Madras Mail*, February 6, 1897 pp. 7
21 Ibid., 5.
22 Ibid., 25.
23 Ibid., 14.
24 Ibid.
25 Ibid., 28.
26 Ibid., 55–56.
27 In light of Govindacharya's agenda in the three lectures, we can say that the more well-known books mentioned above, *The Divine Wisdom of the Dravida Saints* (1902a), *The Holy Lives of the Alvars* (1902b), and *Mazdaism in the Light of Vishnuism* (1913), are intended not only to inform readers about his own Srivaisnava tradition, but also to provide evidence in support of his thesis on the intellectual and spiritual meeting of India and the West on a terrain fair to both. At the end of his career, Govindacharya published *A Metaphysique of Mysticism Vedically Viewed* (1923), a collection of twelve studies on a range of instances of the mystical, including the divine–human relationship, love, Krishna, mystical experience, Buddhism and mysticism, Dravidian (Tamil, south Indian) mysticism, and Vedanta and Persian mysticism.
28 Seal 1899: i–ii.
29 Ibid., iii.
30 Ibid., v.
31 Ibid., v–vi.
32 Ibid., vi–vii.
33 Ibid., vii.
34 Ibid., viii.
35 Ibid., ix–x.
36 Ibid., ix.
37 Ibid., vi. See also Amita Chatterjee 2015.
38 Seal 1899, xi. In the course of the actual comparison, he covers a wide range of themes, first within Hindu traditions and then in selective comparisons. Even today his list would be useful in Hindu–Christian studies: (1) the doctrine of the God-head, with reference to the four-fold emanation series, and the classification of the ultimate principles or categories in the cosmogonic order; (2) the doctrine of the God-head with reference to the Trinity; (3) the relation of the universal to the individual soul; (4) the idea of salvation; (5) the universality of salvation by faith; (6) the relation of faith to righteousness and to philosophical knowledge; (7) the relation of grace to righteousness and merit; (8) the relation of the universal to the individual will, or divine government and human freedom; (9) the essentials of faith and divine worship, with the relation of religion to morality, or of the love of God to the love of the human; (10) the doctrine of repentance; (11) the question of social life versus monachism; (12) the relation of the human to the divine in the God-man, and the nature of his body (ibid., 32) He explains how he will proceed regarding such an array of topics: "I will briefly treat each topic, when it comes into view, from the historical as well as the comparative point of view. Usually I give the history of the Indian doctrine or practice, merely suggesting the points of similarity or contrast in the Christian history" (ibid.).

39 Ibid., 4.
40 Including select Upanisads, the Gita, the Brahma Sutras, and some particular Vedantic readings; the Sandilya Sutras, the Narada Pancharatra and Narada Bhakti Sutras, and the Markandeya Purana; the Laws of Manu; several Puranic texts.
41 Ibid., 102.
42 Ibid.
43 Ibid., 102–103.
44 Bhattacharyya 2011 [1929], 103.
45 Ibid., 104.
46 Ibid., 105–106.
47 Ibid., 107.
48 Ibid.
49 Ibid., 108.
50 Edward Hulmes records the intention of the donor, H. N Spalding: "It is a condition of the Gift that the purpose of the professorship shall be to build up in the University of Oxford a permanent interest in the great religions and ethical systems (alike in their individual, social, and political, aspects) of the East, whether expressed in philosophic, poetic, devotional, or other literature, in art, history, and in social life and structure, to set forth their development and spiritual meaning, and to interpret them by comparison and contrast with each other and with the religions and ethics of the West and in any other appropriate way, with the aim of bringing together the world's great religions in closer understanding, harmony, and friendship; as well as to promote co-operation with other Universities, bodies, and persona, in East and West which pursue the like ends, which purpose is likely to be furthered by the establishment of a Professorship, which would in the natural course normally be held by persons of Asian descent" (2002: 113–114).
51 Radhakrishnan 1936: 18.
52 Ibid., 18–19.
53 Ibid., 19.
54 Ibid., 21.
55 Ibid., 27.
56 Ibid., 30.
57 Ibid., 31.
58 Radhakrishnan 1939: 348.
59 Zaehner 1953: 4–5.
60 Ibid., 4.
61 Ibid., 4–5.
62 Ibid., 8.
63 Ibid., 8–9.
64 Ibid., 17.
65 Ibid.
66 Matilal 2002b: 60–63.
67 Ibid., 61.
68 Matilal 2002a: 351.
69 Ibid., 352.
70 Ibid., 355.
71 Ibid., 356.

72 The text is the inaugural address delivered at the opening of the Centre for Indian and Inter-Religious Studies, Rome, on September 15, 1977.
73 Matilal 2002c:, 162.
74 Ibid., 163.
75 Ibid., 164–165.
76 From "Transcendental Philosophy," Murty 1973: 166–167
77 Ibid., 83.
78 Ibid., 107.
79 Krishna 2014.
80 Ibid., 77.
81 Ibid.
82 Ibid.
83 Ibid., 82.
84 Ibid.
85 Ibid., 83. See also Krishna 2001.
86 Sharma 2005: 25.
87 Ibid.
88 Ibid., 32.
89 Ibid., 33.
90 Ibid., 91.
91 Ibid., 247–248.
92 Ibid., 250, citing Smith 2004: 29.
93 Sharma 2005: 250.
94 Ibid., 254.
95 Patil 2001: 186–187.
96 Ibid., 189.
97 Ibid., 190.
98 I summarize points made in Malhotra 2016: 357–373.
99 Ibid., 373.
100 Ibid., 380.
101 Ibid.

Lecture Three

How the study of religions can rejuvenate Hindu–Christian studies

Rethinking our study of religions, Christianity, and Hinduism

In the third and final lecture, I shift my gaze to the modern Western (and largely North American) context, in order to ask how the study of religion, religions, theology, and Hinduism and Christianity, in the contemporary academic context, may show a way forward for both Hindus and Christians.

This third lecture argues for the constructive role of religious studies in the work of a rejuvenated Hindu–Christian studies. The modern discipline of the study of religions has often been cast as unfriendly to faith and believing communities and their theologies. Suspicions are not without cause, given uneasy relations between believers and scholars, which in the West reach back to the Enlightenment. For a very long time, dis-ease and misunderstanding have vexed relations between believing Christians and scholars of religion; Hindu dis-ease at modern scholarship is a predictable extension of an older tension. Even today, being a believing Christian or Hindu may slow the career of a young scholar, given the expectation that an explicit faith operative in a scholar's work may detract from that work as scholarship by hampering the detached freedom of such work, and tailoring it rather to an imposed purpose that is both extrinsic to the work and likely to misshape how it proceeds, what is studied, and what results are counted as relevant. Such points are often debated, and in this lecture I do not intend here to make a contribution to the general issues involved.

The study of religion has arisen and flourished in the modern West, where for centuries Christianity has been the privileged religion. But this privilege is accompanied too by sharp and uncomfortable added attention, study that is particularly critical of Christianity, and has done much to erode its authority and privilege. The historical/critical method and its postmodern variants are today the norm, and no religious text is exempt from scrutiny. Religious intellectuals in the West have learned to deal with this critique, either by rising to the standards of that criticism and prioritizing what can be historically proven, or by rethinking where and how the truth of scripture and religious practice will appear. In this context, the study of India is distanced from an overly Christian perspective, and new scholarship on every detail of Indian history, culture, and religion serves to broaden and enrich how we think of its religions. Histories of colonialism and orientalism dispel the myth of Western objectivity regarding India.

But I do want to propose that even while the modern study of religion cannot of itself provide the substance of Hindu–Christian studies, which, as I have argued, is distinguished by the element of faith, its methods and questions do expand the options for a new era in Hindu–Christian learning. Historical and philosophical studies of both religions have proliferated, and scholars have robustly questioned the settled stories traditional believers, like other human beings, tell about themselves and the others, outsiders, who play a role in those stories. New information accumulating, and new methods and perspectives, from within traditions and outside them, are changing how we think about our religions, how we imagine and deconstruct their internal unity. Even the turn to popular religion, respected now for its distance from traditions scripturally and doctrinally described, unsettles standard narratives and lineages of authority.

None of this means that the study of religions, with its sub-fields of the study of Hinduism and the study of Christianity, easily becomes tantamount to the new Hindu–Christian studies. More and new study of either religion, plus a clearer and more honest recognition of the history of both religions in their interactions, does not add up to the desired renewed Hindu–Christian studies. Hindu–Christian studies is a kind of theological exchange, and no quantity of scholarly inquiry adds up to theology if faith is still missing. The scholarly study of religion tends to rule out extrinsic and external sources of authority. But it may at the same time also rule out the possibility of substantive religious values: revelation, inspiration, truth, etc. Even if the academy has become more comfortable with the fact of believing scholars, there is still a risk that the committed perspective of a believer is counted out, reduced to an object of study rather than featured as a living voice pertinent to the professional identity of the scholars involved.

And yet, the academy is becoming more comfortable with the fact of believing scholars. While great priority is still given to academic rigor and discipline, the modern study of religion also shares the wider academic skepticism about the very ideal of a free, detached display of reason. No one is without bias, and a faith bias is not necessarily any worse than other biases. Even if biases are deeply engrained, few will argue forthrightly that the intellectual production of the West is inherently superior to that of other cultures. In our post-colonial, post-orientalist age, the work of uncovering and critiquing Christian scholarship and Western intellectualism is accompanied by a denial of their superiority. Scholarship has leveled the playing field, so to speak: it has created freer spaces for Hindu and Christian scholars but also made both Hindus and Christians uncomfortable by privileging the perspectives of outsiders. Modern academic work has also made us more self-conscious regarding the inside and outsider perspectives. While the privileges accruing to either perspective can be exaggerated, attention to this factor matters with respect to how religions are studied, since often enough insiders provide different and often richer contexts for individual beliefs and practices, while outsiders, in their analytic work, see things apart from habitual frames of interpretation and in different contexts, often also in keeping with modern academe's preferences. This dynamic predicts increased tension between insiders and outsiders in today's world, when elite boundaries have eroded, and even non-academic insiders are quite aware of how outsiders are writing about them. In an odd way, both parties to Hindu–Christian studies may find themselves allies in the work of defending truth, tradition, and the substantive value of religious ways of seeing the world.

Many challenges remain, then, even after we acknowledge advances achieved by the modern study of religions. For a moment, though, I wish to stress the positive. Today there are unprecedented new opportunities for the study of Christianity and Hinduism, individually and in detail, in a web of historical connections, and by fairer methods of comparative study. We see a liberative opening up of new approaches that enable us to read differently, critically and imaginatively, the great texts of traditions, while also retrieving and reading lesser studied and sometimes suppressed texts. In turn, new ways have developed that balance textual study with ethnographic work, such that the great books are relocated within the realm of lived religion, without abandoning the traditional virtues of study. Recognition of an irreducible multiplicity of voices now includes, as a tentative good, even the opening of religious identity into related identity matters, including ethnicity, race, and gender. We see today an increasing comfort with scholarship that does not exclude or marginalize the role of a personal, faith-engaged stance in what one studies, such as allows scholars to "come out" as Hindu in the academy, allows Christians – and then

Hindus and others – to be forthright in a new way regarding how Christian identity affects scholarship. And so in academe today, even while there is not parity regarding "being Christian" and "being Hindu," we have the happy prospect of more scholars who are admittedly Hindu, and their confessions of faith, as it were, may be discerned to have a positive role in their scholarship. Even short of that goal, we also have more scholars who choose not to conceal their faith, but stand ready to engage in fresh conversations with religious intellectuals in other traditions.

A note on the widened academic possibilities today

It is not unimportant to note that there are now more than ever before good opportunities for the study of Hinduism in academic venues, and with a considerable number of the scholars involved self-identifying as Hindu. Let us recollect several of the changes taking place by noting the unprecedented array of options available for writing and publishing. I will use the example of the American Academy of Religion, where two features notable today are pertinent.

First, there is much more comfort than in the past with confessional scholars who, while striving to uphold high standards, are forthright about speaking from a confessional perspective. Scholarly objectivity is no longer seen as necessarily entailing the lack of, or silence about, any confessional commitments one might bring to academic work. There is no consensus, of course, but scholars who are believers need not, today, feel marginal or excluded. The American Academy of Religion (henceforth AAR) and similar academic conferences host a variety of venues in which Hinduism can be discussed, papers presented, beyond the range of theological and philosophical, sociological and historical sections and groups in which religion outside the West is sometimes taken up. Thus we have the long-running Religion in South Asia Section, the Hinduism Group, the North American Hinduism Group, etc., and also the allied Dharma Academy of North America, which meets in tandem with the AAR every year. The Society for Hindu–Christian Studies, of which I was the first president about twenty-five years ago, also meets at the annual meeting of the AAR. In recent years this Society has used its two panels, when possible, to feature historical-textual-philosophical-theological topics in one, and contemporary and sociological-anthropological topics in the other. Hinduism is studied in a variety of ways today, by Hindus and non-Hindus, and, despite the ordinary range of academic disagreements, largely without great controversy. Given its location largely in the United States, the membership has always been predominantly Christian, but likewise, in the sessions and in the allied *Journal of Hindu–Christian Studies*, continual efforts have been made to make the Society meaningfully and fairly a matter of Hindu–Christian studies in the stronger sense used in this book. It has as far as possible included a balance of Hindu and Christian presenters.

While the AAR is just one example, it is the world's largest and most influential meeting of scholars of religion. The diverse and complex learning that occurs at such conventions cumulatively makes the case that the study of Hinduism has made advances and consolidated a real and important position in the modern academy. As for publishing, there is evidence for the settled and more equal place for Hindu perspectives in academic publishing. Several journals are notable in their dedication to publishing in the area of Hinduism. The *International Journal of Hindu Studies* and the *Journal of Hindu Studies* are refereed journals with a good track record (the former of nearly twenty years, the latter of nearly a decade), featuring a wide range of studies on all topics related to Hinduism within the context of the latest developments in South Asian studies, religious studies, and related fields. The *Journal of Vaishnava Studies*, which, too, is over twenty years old, can also be mentioned here, as offering valuable thematic issues on topics of academic interest with historical and contemporary import, and essays written very often by authors of Hindu background. These journals are distinguished by first-rate scholarship that is also characteristically sympathetic study, modelling scholarship that is respectful, and constructive rather than deconstructive. We can also mention, finally, the many publishing possibilities with presses such as Oxford University Press, the important work over decades at the State University of New York Press, and the Routledge Hindu Studies Series, which now lists over thirty titles – including the present volume.

Debating the study of religions: which kind of study?

The set of Hindu and Christian religious intellectuals who study each other's religions will thankfully include many respected scholars who study *about* religion and religions, and this is for the better. But at its core ought to be the set of religious intellectuals who in their research address factors of faith and tradition, community and community boundaries, and also engage in religious practices appropriate to the religions as understood and responded to. These engaged and committed practitioner scholars will have a strong sense of the inner life and obligations of their communities, even when they are also open to engaging their religious others. While it is controversial to say that the core community for Hindu–Christian scholars is comprised of believing Hindus and believing Christians, and while it would be impractical to monitor in intrusive ways who is a believer and practitioner or not, the narrowing is in principle worth its cost. The converse marginalization of believers will not achieve the goal of rejuvenating Hindu–Christian studies, nor find a way around the impasses that have diminished the field in our time. It is therefore necessary to say more about forms of the study of religions that are conducive to the reflective multi-dimensionality appropriate to Hindu–Christian studies.[1]

Again employing a lecturer's necessary shorthand, I characterize this kind of study by an appeal to Gavin Flood's 2013 *The Truth Within: A History of Inwardness in Christianity, Hinduism, and Buddhism* and then to his earlier exchange with Nancy Levene on the nature of the study of religion. In the book, Flood reflects on the theme of the inner self and inwardness, and it serves as a fine example of comparative work, this time in three traditions, treated respectfully and studied attentively. It also serves to justify the presupposition, not always welcomed in academic circles, that there are substantive commonalities across religious and cultural boundaries. Part One consists of five chapters: "Prayer and Vision in the Christian Middle Ages"; "Inwardness as Mystical Ascent" in the Christian context; "Inwardness and Visual Contemplation" and a "Philosophy of Inwardness" in the Hindu context; and, regarding Buddhism, "Inwardness without Self." Balancing the broad view with selectivity in his study, Flood skillfully narrates across the three traditions the story of interiority and practices cultivating it.

The idea that interiority is an important constituent value in almost all religions is not controversial, but Flood notes too that attending to this interiority opens up a realm of comparative study genuinely alternative to the modes of socially and historically restricted modes now current. By highlighting interiority, Flood reminds us of Govindacharya: to be sure, a world away and in different form, but with a similar sensitivity to metaphysical and spiritual commonalities. With a contemporary rigor, Flood retrieves "inner comparison," as it were, and thereby grounds a certain kind of comparative study that does not focus merely on the social and the political, nor on the fate of the individualized and privatized self. Flood does not speculate at length on the implications of his retrieval of interiority. He does not appeal to the reader to retrieve that interiority for herself or himself, and perhaps *The Truth Within* aims simply to reopen a closed channel of comparative study, the fact and implications of interiority as a useful heuristic category but also a reality in multiple traditions. In this, again, he is echoing themes we saw arising, from a quite different perspective, in Govindacharya's 1897 lectures.

Which form of religious studies?

In this light we can better appreciate Flood's more sharply focused exchange with Nancy Levene, "Reflections on Tradition and Inquiry in the Study of Religion" in the *Journal of the American Academy of Religion* (henceforth *JAAR*) 2006 thematic discussion, "On the Future of the Study of Religion in the Academy." In his piece, Flood insists that the study of religion ought not be counted simply as one of the social sciences; nor need it privilege only those speaking from outside the traditions studied. It is also a field of the humanities, and also a field in which participants in the traditions studied can write with perfect respectability. This is crucial to the future of the field:

> If Religious Studies is to survive into the future … it needs to be able to discuss and articulate areas of shared concern in forms of language, whereby different world religions and discreet subject-specific areas can communicate and illuminate each other.[2]

Mutual illumination – Sharma's reciprocal illumination – is crucial to Hindu–Christian studies as well, and requires that we

> overcome the inadequate choice of using either problematic universal categories in understanding religions or a relativistic reversion to purely area-specific study which relegates the study of "religions" to departments of Anthropology, Sociology, or whatever and excludes theologies of traditions from the secular academy.

Countering such (intended or unintended) strategies of diminution, we need rather to promote religious studies as "a field of inquiry that gives hospitality to traditions and their self-representations, allows for discussion across subdisciplines such as the Anthropology of Religion, Sociology of Religion, Philology, and so on, and interfaces with a public discourse." To this list I would add discussion with believing intellectuals in various traditions. By such hospitality, religious studies becomes able to embrace "a diversity of kinds of reasoning (or rational inquiry founded on both secular and religious presuppositions) along with the ability to speak across disciplines."[3] Flood thus argues "for a Religious Studies not only or primarily as the social scientific study of religion but as an arena that gives legitimacy to traditions' self-inquiry within a framework of rational discourse."[4] He speaks against "a naturalist or eliminative reductionism" that in essence explains away the first-order discourses of believers, and against "a cultural reductionism" that reduces the meaning of religion to "a politics of representation and structures of power."[5]

Flood is well aware of the current resistance to a narrow focus on the textuality of traditions and the doctrines of traditions, but he believes that good scholarship need not be driven by skepticism about traditions' own explanations of themselves. Attention to elite texts need not amount to a merely textual manner of scholarship. Rather, great texts, carefully read, shed light on historical and cultural frameworks, and show how those text-focused traditions were creating the patterns of living and framework of values within which people live their lives in particular historical communities.[6] Flood thus opens a space for religious people's own self-interpretation even in their adherence to tradition.[7] Rehabilitated in a way that allows for second-order (theological) reflection, religious studies can then "function as an arena that allows the self-articulation of traditions to reflect upon themselves, that allows for second-order discourse, while also offering a third-order discourse that reflects upon and offers corrective readings of traditions' self-descriptions."[8] It is this kind of religious studies, open to theological concerns even if not fully guided by the faith concerns of theology, that is required for Hindu–Christian studies to be a viable field today.

Nancy Levene's response to Flood is also illuminating. In an attentive though critical response, she spotlights Flood's defense of theology as an academic discipline and disputes the value of privileging theology. After all, she says, every manner of knowledge faces the same dangers of reductionism and exclusion that Flood is describing. Insofar as theology is an academic discipline, its problems are not special; insofar as its defenders detect unique features in theology, they are stepping outside the academic realm. Flood inadvertently maintains unfruitful dichotomies merely repeated, and his defense of theological learning still polarizes the issues around scholarship in a usual manner, as if to insist, "Religious studies is to accept theology as long as theology (as both a second-order and, potentially, a third-order discourse) heeds the standards of 'rational discourse.'"[9] But this presumes unquestioningly the concept of rationality being debated by those who want theology included and those who argue for its exclusion. Neither Flood's "three reasons"[10] for admitting religiously based standpoints to religious studies nor "his conception of religion as a culturally specific form of human practice and reasoning organized around sacred texts" offers theorists in religion anything new with which to tackle the problem of the theology–religious studies split.[11] So while his concerns are legitimate, his appeals do not change the situation.

Levene even suggests that Flood may even be regressing to what she terms an "Eliadian view" of a "dialogue between traditions focused on their 'central values,' accessed by attending to the (perhaps secret) meaning of religious texts and not just their accessible, public history and 'sociological, economic, or political contexts.'"[12] We have seen that earlier scholars from the West (such as de Nobili and Bouchet) and in India (such as Govindacharya and Radkakrishnan, among others) insist that there is at stake a deeper wisdom not reducible to such external contexts, but Levene does not see this as a positive development.[13] In his brief rejoinder, Flood reaffirms that there are minimal requirements of rationality, not only those of any given cultural moment, but such as are "recognizable across histories and continents" – universals that seem to me to have some spiritual as well as intellectual dimensions. He gives the example of his own study of the premodern Indian philosopher Abhinavagupta, who uses "the terminology of his own tradition" and addresses the "problematics of his own philosophical world." But it is still true that "his lucid argument and processes of reasoning are immediately recognizable to anyone who can read him."[14] This non-reductive "recognizability" is essential to any study of the past that can be deemed worthwhile in the present – including Hindu–Christian studies.

In the same *JAAR* roundtable, a similarly collegial exchange between Jose Cabezón and William Schweiker highlights the need to include insider voices in the study of religion. In his essay "The Discipline and Its Other: The Dialectic of Alterity in the Study of Religion," Cabezón comments on the distinctive place of Asian religions in the academy as our "other":

> My sense is that because of both the demographic and ideological hegemony of (especially Protestant) Christianity in the academy, there is still a very real sense in which non-Christian religions (and especially nonwestern religions) continue to occupy for European and American intellectuals a preeminent position in the hierarchy of otherness.

These religions demand attention because, as it were, they are "other-squared," an otherness accentuated by various strategies that largely separate the scholarly from perspectives of faith and practice.[15] In resistance to this habitual tendency, some scholars reject the dichotomy of "insider" vs. "scholarly," and accept the fact that some scholarly discourses are close "to what we term theology." Tradition-founded thinking can further even the most scholarly investigations; academic discourses can be helpful intellectual contributions to thinking within religious communities. Scholars moving beyond the insider–outsider divide are willing to identify "themselves – or, I should say, ourselves – under such rubrics as Buddhist, Hindu, and/or comparative theology." Moreover,

> there is no reason why the academy should not make room for non-Christian religious/constructive work that is (to invoke the "password") critical, especially since Christian varieties of this same discourse have been an integral part of an organization like the AAR since its inception.[16]

Cabezón thus confirms the benefits of more and not less theology in the academy, provided we draw on more traditions and not fewer. A robust and renewed Hindu–Christian studies, as an academic and faith-grounded discipline, would be a very good example of this progressive inclusion.

In his response, Schweiker notes with approval four trends detected by Cabezón: "1. pluralism; 2. the challenge of religious believers to academics; 3. the self-disclosure of scholar's religious identities; and 4. the movement to the institutionalization of non-Western theologies." Moreover, Schweiker says, "The way academics have defined Themselves against some Other is being transformed even as the lines of loyalty – to the guild and/or to a religious tradition – are being negotiated anew."[17] He recognizes all of this as progress in the study of religion. But Schweiker, to an extent echoing Levene's cautions regarding Flood's proposal, adds that we must not "repeat the problems of the past by assuming that the 'dialectic of alterity' is answered by merely replacing Christian with non-Christian sources. What is needed is a multi-sourced and multidimensional form of thinking," not simply more theologies in their narrow, one-tradition form.[18]

Cabezón agrees that "merely replacing Christian with non-Christian sources" is hardly the solution we seek. Openness to alternate forms of theory "should not devolve into knee-jerk inclusivism." Rather, "we should resort to non-Christian theories not because they are non-Christian, and not because they are religious, but because, quite simply, they illuminate the phenomenon that is being subjected to scrutiny – to put it more bluntly, because they work."[19] This learning is driven in part by its own deep intellectual value, and not just by good intentions or the desire to dialogue. But neither would this exchange work, I take Cabezón to be saying, if we reduce the exchange to an intellectual practice that seeks immunity from matters of faith, experience, and practice. In turn, the truly integral balance then requires us to do together the work of studying these traditions in detail, rather than just debating meta-issues; an important site for this work in the academy is a renewed Hindu–Christian studies.

The issues raised in these (and other) essays in the *JAAR* issue are sharpened by two other essays to which I will briefly call attention, by Jenny Daggers and Chakravarthi Ram-Prasad. In her "Thinking 'Religion': The Christian Past and Interreligious Future of Religious Studies and Theology" (2010), Jenny Daggers seeks to retrieve a humane study of religion. Noting the shifting place of Christianity in the study of religion, she argues that the pertinent academic task is not directly about Christianity, but about rediscovering the place of particularity within the frame of varying constructions of theology and religious studies. In the abstract for her essay Daggers maps three attitudes toward Christianity latent in varying modes of the study of religion: "The category 'religion' is a tripartite, emergent from Christian theology during modernity, as Christianity increased, transcended, and diminished, and persistent in contemporary religious studies and Christian theology." Later, she explains:

> "Religion as Christianity increased" belongs to Christian theology, and has also been influential on emergent religious studies; "religion as Christianity transcended" is the mark of some liberal theologies, whereas "religion as Christianity transcended or diminished" belongs to religious studies in its modernist and contemporary forms.[20]

So too, in accord with today's postmodern and postcolonial "return of religion," the tripartite model itself is filed away as a product of Eurocentric modern Christianity. Not only is Christianity now positioned as "one religion among others," but religious studies engages religious traditions, including Christianity, "in their particularities, rather than in terms of overarching (modernist) categories." (This, I would add, makes it difficult to take seriously the doctrines of traditions, unless the scholar can see that doctrines too are particular, as strategies, statements, and truth.) Conversely, Daggers continues, Christian theology reacts differently to different forms of the study of religion: "while Christianity transcended persists in (pluralist) liberal theologies, religion is repudiated and (particularist) Christianity re-centered in its neo-orthodox strands."[21] Even as Christianity declines in the West and is just "one religious tradition among others," it is now also being noticed also in its global reality, particularly in the "global South," where it is growing in new and vital ways that for new reasons too cannot be boxed in by the categories of the modern West.[22] If the study of religion discards the privilege of Christian theology by claiming to supersede it, that study ironically claims for itself the very notion of progress it wishes to deny to Christian intellectual tradition.[23]

Once such clarifications and cautions are in place, we can notice a remarkable convergence. On the one hand, Daggers suggests, Christian theology is moving

> closer to the terrain of religious studies by, first, attending more closely to the lived religion of Christian faith communities, and, second, developing theologies of religion and comparative theologies which respect the particularity of religious traditions, rather than assuming Christianity to be the destination of all religions.

On the other, "Concurrently, by attending more closely to lived religions in their own terms, religious studies moves closer to the terrain of theology," where particularity is taken with the utmost seriousness and not readily disposed in accord with the work of theory.[24] If so, then the contemporary study of religions allies with chastened, disciplined, and thereby enhanced reimaginings of theology, and provides the productive space for a Hindu–Christian studies that does not shunt faith, tradition, and community to the side.

In a recent essay, "Reading the *Acaryas*: A Generous Conception of the Theological Method," Chakravarthi Ram-Prasad proposes a version of theology that can be distinguished from both the typical, detached academic study of religion, and from the theological work that I characterize as faith seeking understanding. On the one hand, he describes his intellectual work as grounded in scripture and tradition and steeped in respect for these, and on this basis a valid version of Hindu theology: "If a contemporary Hindu theology has to find ways of coming to be today, it can be guided by the *acaryas.* When sacred text is the epistemic foundation for exegesis, we have theology."[25] Readings can still be diverse – as the texts are diverse – and they may be written about in multiple ways; but if there is deference to a scripture and a teaching tradition, "theology" may justly describe the work that is being done. Ram-Prasad steps away from the position of a theologian in one tradition: "I could have written as a theologian born in the Srivaisnava community of Ramanuja, prepared to look and learn about Sankara's Advaita from a Visistadvaita perspective, and be an internal comparative theologian within Clooney's terms." But he prefers to work differently:

> It is not as a member of the Srivaisnava community that I have read either commentator. At the same time, I kept within the terms of what I initially described as theology, which is to take the terms of the discussion to be framed by *sruti* as both starting and ending point of exegesis; in other words, my exegetical exploration did not seek to clarify my understanding of the commentators other than in terms of how they articulated their views through *sruti* (whereas it was always possible to ask, as I did not, philological, literary-critical or historical questions about their interpretations).[26]

This is a sophisticated interpretation and it pays due deference to the frame within which the authors write; but it does not commit the reader to one or another tradition. Rather, there is "a methodological commitment to treating the text as having such unity and conveying meaning, but where such meaning is personal even when the practice of reading is communal." His ideal is not the faith of a community, but that of an intelligent, careful reader. This reading "is not the same as subscribing to the identity-forming potency of that authority; and it therefore does not mean having to adopt precisely the collective doxastic stance of a faith community."[27] Ram-Prasad clearly and elegantly sets forth his arguments for this position, and it is worthy of our consideration. But of itself, it cannot successfully provide the required paradigm for the required scholarship; once its virtues are explained and analyzed, one will either move toward faith-grounded inquiry that remains open to new learning, or recede back into the greater mix of professional but detached academic writing.

Hindu–Christian debates in the contemporary academy

In a manner that I take to be a largely positive development, disagreements between scholars and learned practitioners outside the academy are becoming more visible. In this context it is illuminating to notice a recent instance of disagreement between a Western scholar and learned Hindu intellectuals who, though not professional academics, bring a certain specificity to their criticisms. I am thinking first of the exchange that occurred at the AAR in 2012 regarding Rajiv Malhotra's *Being Different: An Indian Challenge to Western Univeralism*. Malhotra begins his book by explaining that it is about "how

India differs from the West. It aims to challenge certain cherished notions, such as the assumptions that Western paradigms are universal and that the dharmic traditions teach 'the same thing' as Jewish and Christian ones." Nuanced versions of this view reach back, of course, to Govindacharya, Seal, and before, so Malhotra stands in a long line of those with this concern, and asserts a familiar hope

> that the dharmic traditions, while not perfect, offer perspectives and techniques for a genuinely pluralistic social order and a full integration of many different faiths, including atheism and science. … The book hopes to set the terms for a deeper and more informed engagement between dharmic and Western civilizations.[28]

Chapters then get at the substantive issues by a variety of themes, related to ways of engaging difference, yoga and (or vs.) history, kinds of unity depending on Christian faith perspectives and Greek philosophical stances, notions of order and chaos, Sanskrit and its civilizational dimensions, universalism, and modes of ongoing argument. The topics are interesting and useful, and merit careful attention.

Near the end of the book's, Malhotra sums up his hopes for ongoing beneficial debate, if certain conditions are met: "It must take place on a level playing field with the conditions, time and place of engagement set by mutual agreement"; conversion cannot be the intent on either side; the debate will most likely not lead to a "win-win" outcome; the participants' egos must be mastered, to allow for humble exchanges; and finally,

> in addition to their spiritual credentials, the defenders of dharma need to be deeply informed about, and well-versed in, the traditions and theologies of their opponents. Likewise, those representing the Western religions must be open to the possibility of dharma as a serious alternative to their own tradition and worldview.[29]

Despite the language of "opponents," the kind of engagement Malhotra is calling for seems quite compatible with this book's hopes regarding the revival of a fair and fruitful Hindu–Christian learning.

An occasion for testing these possibilities occurred at the AAR in 2012, under the auspices of the Society for Hindu–Christian Studies. Three scholars – Brian Pennington, Jonathan Edelman, and Anantanand Rambachan – responded to the book, and Malhotra responded to them. The report on the event appears in the *Journal of Hindu–Christian Studies* (2013). Bradley Malkovsky, the journal editor, characterizes the panel in this way:

> The three reviewers of *Being Different* in the present volume at first express solidarity with Malhotra and agree that his is an urgent and necessary undertaking, if the distinctiveness of Indian religions and culture is to be taken seriously in the academy and beyond. But all three go on to fault Malhotra for making sweeping and uninformed generalizations about religions, focusing their critique more on Malhotra's presentation of Indian religions than on his presentation of Abrahamic faiths. Malhotra defends himself in a long response, pointing out where he believes himself to be misrepresented or misunderstood and where he finds the three reviewers show deficiency in their own scholarly approach to his work.[30]

All three discussants took seriously Malhotra's points, but fairly enough pointed to a more complex and nuanced view of Hinduism, and resisted the temptation to reduce it to Advaita, or to a vaguely grounded *sanatana dharma*. Hinduism is never so generic as to appear to float above and apart from specific traditions. In other words, the discussants were willing to engage in a conversation about the book, but asked for clarifications in terminology and method, necessary refinements regarding the historical relations between India and the West, Hindus and Christians, and theological clarifications regarding the nature of religious authority, evidence and experience, and the qualifications of individuals who claim to speak for traditions.

In his response, Malhotra sought to defend the value and coherence of a modern Hinduism shaped by science rather than being grounded in the specifics of the premodern traditions:

> Rambachan could make a great contribution to Hindu Studies if he could only recognize the new paradigms emerging in science and religion and accept a broader definition of what Hinduism is and how it relates to contemporary Western thought. Were he to open his eyes to the Western appropriation of Hindu ideas, he might (given his expertise) be able to shed some much needed light on the matter in terms of clarification and correction.[31]

To Pennington, he admits that currently his work is aimed at the Hindu community rather than the scholarly community,[32] and is about contesting the scholarly monopoly on how Hinduism is to be interpreted. To Edelmann, his response was that he does not find significant the complexity of the Christian and Hindu traditions Edelmann stresses, and sees no need to deepen his own relation to some particular tradition of learning in order to be credible. That is to say, his understanding of what it means to be a Hindu religious intellectual was quite different from theirs, in an odd way more polemical but yet too more expectant that diverse views be accepted rather than critiqued. By the end of the evening, some understanding had been achieved, but the gaps regarding what counts as learning regarding Hinduism were all the more pronounced.

But the larger issue of the reinvigoration of Indian and Hindu thought is central to *Being Different*, and Malhotra's intention to promote that renewal – and the related self-defense – can be considered an important contribution to the enabling of a multi-faceted conversation on the topic. The three discussants took the book seriously, and were honest, on target, and correct in offering their criticisms. We are better off because they were in fact willing to discuss the matters with an intellectual who is not a scholar, and who has often showed impatience with, and hostility toward, those who devote their lives to the study of Hinduism. While we may not at first see this uncomfortable argument as a step forward in Hindu–Christian studies, the heated engagement does indicate that a line of communication was for a time opened. As the one who proposed the panel, I believed, and still do, that the boundaries of academia cannot be hard and fast, so as to exclude non-academics from the conversation. Rather, religious intellectuals from outside academe ought on occasion to be welcomed for conversation on issues of mutual concern. Theologians seek to balance such issues, and the difficulties arising are largely worth the trouble. In any case, Malhotra speaks to and for a significant number of Hindus.[33] But it was also clear that further disciplined conversations, able to take up the details of the debated positions in their familiar classical forms, are required to solidify any gains that might have been made in a single evening. Hence the need, I argue, for regular and then habitual practices of Hindu–Christian conversation.

Second, I draw attention to one moment in the debate surrounding Jeffrey Kripal's *Kali's Child*: the response offered by Swami Tyagananda and Pravrajika Vrajaprana in their *Interpreting Ramakrishna* (2010). *Kali's Child* was the first book by Kripal, a distinguished scholar now with many books to his credit. It was controversial in part simply because its topic, a psycho-spiritual-sexual interpretation of the Hindu saint Ramakrishna, was highly sensitive, and in part because of some controverted interpretations Kripal makes in the book. In its first pages, Kripal argues that Ramakrishna's erotic mysticism is inseparable from his homosexuality, and as such is a key crucial to explaining events in his life that were "profoundly, provocatively, scandalously erotic." To show this, he aims at "a historically accurate, psychologically nuanced reading of the Hindu Tantra as it was practiced by Ramakrishna." Tantra, more than Vedanta, was the key element in his spiritual practice. As a homosexual,

> he could not be forced to complete the Tantric ritual of *maithuna* or "sexual intercourse," with a woman, for example, not because he had somehow transcended sex (the traditional claim) but because the ritual's heterosexual assumptions seriously violated the structure of his own homosexual desires.

Even to the end of his life, Ramakrishna remained "a lover not of sexually aggressive women or even of older men but of young, beautiful boys, those 'pure pots,' as he called them, that could hold the 'milk' of his divine love." Kripal's overall argument is that "Ramakrishna was a conflicted, unwilling, homoerotic Tantrika who was as skilled at refashioning and realizing the meanings of the Hindu Tantra as he was uncomfortable in its symbolic world."[34] This of course is a controversial reading of the saint and a difficult application of psychoanalytic assessments, and it elicited strong negative responses in India.

The controversy was uncomfortable and generated some nasty sentiments unfair to Kripal But it also created the conditions for a rich exchange between Kripal and Swami Tyagananda and Pravrajika Vrajaprana of the Ramakrishna Order. Putting aside the heated rhetoric around *Kali's Child* to offer a challenging but scholarly and detailed critique, they first review the history of the reception of Ramakrishna within and outside the Vedanta community. In the course of that survey they notice and assess the conditions under which insiders and outsiders will unsurprisingly hold and defend different views of the saint – while they also hold that no one need have drawn Kripal's conclusions. Then they analyze the specific points made by Kripal, criticize his translations and interpretations, and dispute the idea that the Order was hiding the truth about Ramakrishna. Their comments are strong, but like Kripal, they refrain from *ad hominem* attacks, and carry on the debate in a way that is both intellectually and spiritually attuned. Kripal is not superior as an outsider (nor did he claim to be), and Vrajaprana and Tyagananda are neither to be dismissed nor favored simply because they are insiders to the tradition in question. Kripal, Vrajaprana, and Tyagananda are all concerned about text, translation, context; all are concerned about the right and wrong applications of theory; they are all mindful of historical precedents and the influence of historical details; they are aware of insider–outsider issues, but avoid arguments that privilege the one over the other. And, in the midst of all this, their positions manifest interestingly contrasting theological views that reach to the heart of the matter. Kripal, of a Catholic Christian background, works with an incarnational sensitivity more interested in the flesh-and-blood historical Ramakrishna, while Vrajaprana and Tyagananda, the Hindus, focus on the message and wisdom of the *avatara*; to them, the flesh-and-blood details of Ramakrishna's life and psyche are, if not negligible, of less import. One might here make a contrast between different Christologies, which view Christ "from below" and "from above," thus beginning with either his humanity or his divinity. By my reading, a knowledge of such parallels – Christian, Vedantic – would help to situate the views of Kripal, Tyagananda, and Vrajaprana on foundations that are not entirely set by the politics of colonial and post-colonial disputation. Once the importance of a theological perspective is admitted, therefore, we have before us a difficult, but mature and ultimately beneficial, form of Hindu–Christian studies.

The debates around *Being Different* and *Kali's Child* raise similar questions about the right balance between scholarship and faith perspectives, faith perspectives which themselves encode varying attitudes toward the roles of critical thinking and responsibility to communities. In light of the importance of the issues raised, the largely constructive nature of the written exchanges, and the fact itself of a kind of peer conversation between academic scholars and learned religious intellectuals, I am hopeful that even on the most difficult matters, we can move forward. Ideally, habits of constructive conversation can defuse misunderstandings before research reaches publication, but even the more advanced forms of Hindu–Christian learning will still need to leave room for disagreements that are actually disclosive of matters both sides care about.

Integral learning: from the study of religions to Hindu–Christian studies

In the first part of this third lecture, I stressed the positive contribution made by the study of religions in creating new and promising possibilities for Hindu–Christian studies in our 21st century. The contemporary academy, in all its diversity, is reshaping how Christians and Hindus study their own religion and the other and breaking up old ways of portraying self and other, potentially preparing a space that is both challenging and congenial to Hindu–Christian studies. The modern academy breathes new life into the field of Hindu–Christian studies by leading us beyond the impasse of a Christian learning that engages its religious other but also undermines that other, and of a Hindu learning that is more ready to seriously engage Western philosophy than what is in many cases actually Hinduism's closer kin, Christian theology.

But, as I have cautioned more than once, the study of religions in and of itself, as a broad field, cannot be assumed to facilitate Hindu–Christian studies. Given that the historical and intellectual forces undercutting Christian intellectual hegemony will also tend to undercut any faith perspective, one cannot simply presume that the study of religions will favor Hindu views or automatically sustain an intellectual and spiritual community of Hindu and Christian scholars. Study will advance, surely, but other intellectual values and habits – the delicate balance of faith and community, critique without reductionism, scholarly learning that respects but is not reduced to norms common in the West – are balances and critiques that require care. Insiders to the two traditions, engaging in the work of faith and reason and encountering the other with the values and resources of faith and reason, will need to keep working together in fashioning an intellectual exchange akin to the work of Flood discussed earlier in this lecture.

Notes

1 Here too, I offer reflections aimed at clarifying the status of a theologically grounded Hindu–Christian studies, and do not imagine myself preempting wider scholarship on religious studies today. For important and wider reflections, see Brown and Cady 2002, and Nehring and Schmidt-Leukel 2016.
2 Flood 2006: 48.
3 Ibid.
4 Ibid.
5 Ibid., 49.
6 Ibid., 52.
7 Ibid., 54.
8 ibid., 56.
9 Levene 2006: 60.
10 Earlier on Flood had identified these: "A number of assumptions are operative in such an understanding, three of which I shall outline. First, religion only exists within cultures (as, one might add, does the study of religion); second, text is the model of culture; and third, inquiry into religions is dialogical and entails an encounter of different kinds of reasoning" (Flood 2006: 51).
11 Levene 2006: 60.
12 Ibid.
13 Ibid.

14 Flood 2006: 64–65.
15 Cabezón 2006a: 27.
16 Ibid., 34.
17 Schweiker 2006: 41.
18 Ibid,. 41–43.
19 Cabezón 2006b: 46.
20 Daggers 2010: 963.
21 Ibid., 961.
22 Ibid., 962.
23 Ibid., 964.
24 Ibid.
25 Ram-Prasad 2014: 108.
26 Ibid., 109.
27 Ibid., 110.
28 Malhotra 2011: 2.
29 Ibid., 339.
30 Malkovsky 2013: 1.
31 Malhotra 2013: 29.
32 Ibid., 44.
33 I include this exchange in order to honor the seriousness of it, and its illuminating nature, since the respondents were conscientious in taking seriously the book and the issues raised. But I do not commend the aftermath, the flood of emails and online exchanges condemning the respondents for presuming to pose critical questions.
34 Kripal 1998: 2–3

Epilogue

Retrieving the delicate balance of Hindu–Christian studies

Hindu–Christian studies as a primarily theological project

In the preceding pages we have made progress in identifying key problems and, implicitly, the goal of a learning that is integrated in one's own tradition, and cultivated in such a way as to remain truly open to the other. Without idealizing or damning the past, Hindu and Christian scholars need to move beyond the imperfect and in some ways very unfortunate history of our relations, recalibrate our mutual learning for a dramatically different 21st century, and become literate in the modern academic study of history and new methods in the study of religions and theology. While alert to the difficulties and challenges pressing in on Hindu--Christian studies from all sides, we need to avoid letting the ideal and the perfect – ever elusive – prevent us from doing the good together that we can manage to do. We need to refuse to reduce our new learning to matters of politics and power. In the third lecture, I sought to move beyond the partial and uneven learning evident in the Christian study of Hinduism and Hindu study of the Christian West. For that purpose I surveyed the state of the study of religions today, and acknowledged its great potential, its role in drawing religious intellectuals and their traditions into a fairer and neutral space, where we can expect a new flourishing of Hindu–Christian studies. I also suggested that the study of religions, its many virtues notwithstanding, is more beneficial when it is constructively open to insider views, not separating faith and reason in order to intentionally or unintentionally neglect the former, but rather allowing the spiritual to remain in vital connection with the intellectual.

This epilogue reaches beyond the three lectures, to speak further on several issues that arose piecemeal throughout. If, as I have suggested, what is at stake can best be described as the quest for a theological grounding and a theological disposition conducive to a Hindu–Christian studies that is intellectually and spiritually compelling on both sides, then we need a theological renewal: the restoration of the practice of theology, as a discipline that does flourish in both the Christian and Hindu contexts, provided attention is also paid to the required spiritual-intellectual grounding.

And so we need to talk about theology more directly than I did in the three lectures. In *Comparative Theology* (2010) I explained theology as faith seeking understanding, proposed a version of non-reductive comparison, and distinguished comparative theology from comparative religion, the history of religions, the theology of religions, and interreligious dialogue. I need not repeat those distinctions here. But given my emphasis in the three lectures on the necessity of keeping one's balance if respectful and mutual learning is to occur, it will be worthwhile here to reflect on the virtues necessary to successful interreligious learning and thus also to Hindu–Christian studies, distancing it from solipsism and intellectual violence.

In our religiously diverse context, "theology" ought not to be described as merely a Christian mode of study. How theology is done will vary from tradition to tradition, but at its core it needs to maintain the balance adverted to many times in the preceding pages: "faith seeking understanding," an intellectual work that is grounded in the truths and values of Christian and Hindu traditions; that remains engaged in the life and practice of the respective religious communities, even while committed to learning anew across the religious divide. A contemporary vital theology resists the notion that religious diversity and academic neutrality render strong claims about truth and value impossible. And yet, though grounded in tradition and committed to truth in its particular cognitive and practical forms, it is also resolutely open, resisting too tight a binding to any given viewpoint.

In turn, "comparative theology" is a signal version of that deeply grounded and deeply open theology. It honors diversity and tradition, openness and truth, and requires that both traditions involved, that of the student and that of the tradition studied, are key to the learning process which rejects an imposition of an alien frame and meaning on the other tradition studied, and also rejects a turn to a relativism that dishonors both traditions. Comparative theology counters the tendency to retreat into private spirituality or into a defensive assertion of truth or a mode of study that is blind and deaf to faith. It is hopeful about the value of a learning that, though complex, is fruitful. Indeed, the theological confidence that we can respect diversity and tradition, that we can study traditions in their particularity and receive truth in this way, in order to know God better, is at the core of comparative theology, and comparative theology provides a good frame for the work of Hindu–Christian studies.

Comparative theology has a close relationship to Hindu–Christian studies. Indeed, my own study of Hinduism as a Christian and my gradual articulation of comparative theology as a field have advanced hand in hand. I started using the terminology of comparative theology precisely in order to defend the theological nature of my study of Hinduism. That I have always detected an easy and deep resonance between Hindu and Christian truths, virtues, and practices has helped shape my confidence in comparative theology as an artful and creative process that, while it has a history, is not determined by that history to go forward in only one way.[1] The hopeful view I have proposed of theological openness and mutual enrichment might certainly have been confirmed by examples of Jewish– or Muslim– or Buddhist–Christian studies, but the nature of the learning, its possibilities and limits, would also surely have worked out differently in those spaces of study.

Virtues essential to comparative theology

The intellectual work of comparative theology and Hindu–Christian studies is practical as well as a matter of ideas; and it is imperative to be forming persons capable of working in this field. This practice requires a mature – or (ever-)maturing – interiority, to foster rootedness in one tradition while cultivating deeper openness to another. Although scholarly expertise – linguistic skills, historical awareness, the ability to read critically – is indispensable, interreligious theological learning must be a transformative learning indebted to the religious other; grounded and open, it learns to "see inside" that other tradition. Even heavily textual work – translations, the study of scholastic systems, the tracing of lines of thought down through commentaries, the decipherment of ritual and moral codes – requires the ability to keep learning from the other, and writing in a way that discloses rather than obscures.

This practice can be done well or poorly. To do it well, we must pay attention to its key virtues to understand how it ought to be done. As a shorthand for a longer discussion, we can note here a set of essential virtues proposed by Catherine Cornille in *The (Im)possibility of Interreligious Dialogue* (2008): *doctrinal or epistemic humility*: "recognition of one's own fallibility and imperfection … a certain degree of admission of the finite and limited ways in which the ultimate truth has been grasped and expressed within one's own religious teachings, practices, and/or institutional forms";[2] *commitment* to a particular religious tradition: remaining "rooted in the particular religious community from which and for which [we] speak";[3] *interconnection*: "the belief that the teachings and practices of the other religion are in some way related to or relevant for one's own religious tradition … the belief that the teachings and practices of other religions may in some way derive from or point to one's own conception of ultimate reality";[4] *empathy*: "not only an intellectual but also an experiential understanding of the other … a fuller understanding of the religious other must include some grasp of the religious meaning of particular teachings and their impact on the life of believers" such that "they may have an impact on one's own religious tradition";[5] *hospitality*: "the recognition of other religions as potential sources of genuine and distinctive truth … a belief in the possibility of discovering distinctive truth in the other religion," such as "renders dialogue not only possible, but also necessary."[6]

To Cornille's list I have found it helpful to add four related virtues: *risk-taking*: experimenting, allowing the possibility of mistakes, and the possibility of becoming more entangled than one would wish in the other religious tradition; *patience with ambiguity*: because of the experimentation and because of the multiple complexities to be negotiated without hope of a single, governing method or system by which to simplify the complications; *new dwelling*: the ability to become as it were, only imperfectly and analogously yet still deeply, an insider in the other community; *marginality*: we are what we learn and read and write, and so too is required the ability to live on the margins of one's own community, wherein most have not engaged in similar, border-crossing experiments.

Such virtues ought not be slotted as narrowly religion-specific, and can be cultivated across religious boundaries. Any religious intellectual might take to heart St. Paul's exhortation in Philippians 4, "Finally, beloved, whatever is true, whatever is honorable, whatever is just, whatever is pure, whatever is pleasing, whatever is commendable, if there is any excellence and if there is anything worthy of praise, think about these things." Or consider these familiar verses from the *Crest Jewel of Discrimination*:

> Hence the seeker after the Reality of the Atman should take to reasoning, after duly approaching the Guru – who should be the best of the knowers of Brahman, and an ocean of mercy. An intelligent and learned person skilled in arguing in favor of the Scriptures and in refuting counter-arguments against them – one who has got the above characteristics is the fit recipient of the knowledge of the Atman.[7]

Discrimination is required:

> The person who discriminates between the Real and the unreal, whose mind is turned away from the unreal, who possesses calmness and the allied virtues, and who is longing for Liberation, is alone considered qualified to enquire after Brahman.[8]

After elaborating these virtues,[9] the instruction elaborates on calmness (*sama*), self-control (*dama*), withdrawal (*uparati*), forbearance (*titiksa*), faith in God and/or guru (*sraddha*), steady concentration (*samadhana*), and the desire for liberation (*mumuksutva*).[10] With some adjustments, these aids to detachment, focus, and humility will aid us in accomplishing better and more fruitful study. The messages of the *Crest Jewel* and Philippians differ in some ways, but it is clear that the emphasis is on the kind of person who is able to do comparative work properly; we might also look back to Lecture Three and the values argued by Gavin Flood.

My own work as comparative theology and as Hindu–Christian studies

It makes sense then to offer examples of my own writing as first instances of Hindu–Christian learning. Most of my projects are implicitly divided into three parts: a problem arising in the modern and Christian context; the in-depth study of a Hindu text – invariably with commentary, and most often in Sanskrit or Tamil – that promises to shed light on the topic; and a "return" that consciously bears with it the lasting effects of both the Christian starting point and identity, and the Hindu study and the effect it has on me. On some occasions, I begin rather more simply with a Hindu text that I have found important, and let the comparative learning proceed from that study and what it implies. In my writing, I have certainly tried to work on a level field, where admitted Christian starting points and biases do not predetermine the conclusions of the study, where Hindu views are not prejudged, and where the study does not alienate me from my own dispositions in faith. Here are two examples.

In *Divine Mother, Blessed Mother: Hindu Goddesses and the Virgin Mary* (2005b), I argued first that Christian theologians and feminist scholars who debate the nature of the divine, the divine person, God, in relation to the feminine have overly narrowed their work by not paying attention to the Hindu Goddess traditions – well over two thousand years of Goddess worship, documents in art and ritual and in an abundance of texts. To make concrete the possibilities, I chose three Goddess hymns –

great hymns of sixty-one verses (Sanskrit), a hundred (Sanskrit), and a hundred (Tamil) verses, addressed respectively to Sri Laksmi, Mahadevi, and the Apirami Devi. These hymns directly address the Goddess, invite the reader to become a participant in a close reading that is not unlike recitation, and dare the theologian who begins to understand them to appropriate the words as her or his own. In turn, I paired the study of the three Goddess hymns to three Marian hymns, by which to engage the problems of receiving the Goddesses into Christian tradition, and read back and forth. I sought intensity in the reading and the encounter across the margins as it were of the two sets of hymns. The book at its end dwells in the liminal space between traditions, a Catholic notice of the Goddesses yet without either confessing belief in them or denying it.

I aimed for a difficult balance in finishing the book, whereby the momentum would remain on the side of learning, not the ending of learning: "The hymns invite us more urgently to participation, and if we do not want to participate, we may first have to protect ourselves by refusing to engage in the reading, thinking, and understanding that open the way to participation."[11] At the end of such study, I added, some readers may become worshippers of the Goddesses named; others may choose to focus on Mary, the Mother of Jesus, hymns praising her now read in a new way by (Christian) readers mindful of the Goddess hymns. Still others may simply read back and forth without making a choice. For theologians, the opportunities are all the more abundant, important, and difficult. The Catholic theologian is presumably able to feel deep affinity with the traditions of Marian piety, but then reaches beyond the stance of a distant observer into a closer attention to Goddess traditions. The Hindu theologian, perhaps reluctant to encounter the concrete reality of Jesus, now stands near to the Mother of God. Were such learned readers to relate deeply to one tradition but not at all to the other, they would deflate and subvert the work to be done, by reducing what is learned to pre-theological information. The point rather is to dwell in a third space, with necessarily blurred margins, where truth is neither exclusive nor merely plural.

His Hiding Place Is Darkness (2013) was another experiment in comparative reading. I drew first on the biblical Song of Songs, read with the medieval Cistercian sermon-writers Bernard of Clairvaux (on cc. 1–2 of the Song), Gilbert of Hoyland (on cc. 3–4), and John of Ford (on cc. 4–8). I read with it the 9th-century Tamil Hindu classic Tiruvaymoli (Holy Word of Mouth), complemented by the insights of medieval Hindu teachers, Nanjiyar and Nampillai in particular. I focused on what is a major strand in both works, the divine Beloved who withdraws, hides from the human lover. I proposed, in the course of this reading, that the effect of the double reading can be to confuse and isolate the reader, who might find the Beloved in either tradition, acutely feel divine absence in either tradition, but now finds the same dynamics at work in both at the same time. Here too, the classic texts, though from my perspective harmonious, do not anticipate one another, and indeed do not welcome rivals at all. Yet by violating their solitude and exclusivity in reading them together, I strove to take them very seriously. As a reader for a time liminal to both worlds, I had to read such texts apart from their original contexts. Yet as a Catholic theologian, I still intended a home-coming. At the end of *His Hiding Place Is Darkness*, I wrote that this set of exercises sought "a delicate balance between a most intense and particular truth, Jesus the beloved, and the unending drama of aesthetic, dramatic, and true apprehensions that draw us perilously near to other such loves." At issue was a difficult balance: "with a certain theological confidence chastened by the discipline of the theopoetic and the theodramatic, I have managed not to forget that other woman's love and her hiding, hidden beloved, Krishna."[12] It is in the grounded yet open practice of reading, Hindu with Christian, that a true learning occurs such as cannot be acquired elsewhere.

Both books draw deeply on Christian and Hindu traditions of learning. By the time such books are complete, the Hindu sources have been read according to my Christian starting points, and the Christian sources in accord with Hindu sensitivities. As such, they are the fruits of Hindu–Christian study. However, in light of the three lectures, it should be clear that even as complete they require reception in both Christian and Hindu communities, if they are to count as good examples. My reading of my own Christian tradition is singular, since few Christians study Hinduism for as long as I have; so too, no matter how long I have been reading Hindu texts, I cannot credit to myself the perspective of an insider; even if I were to "convert to Hinduism," this is a move that would make more sense to Christians (who value conversions) than to Hindus (who generally do not). So for my work to contribute to a flourishing field of study, it must be received in the two communities, by scholars and students, and in a wider community that becomes used to living in a space overlapping with both communities' faith and traditions and practices. I am relatively hopeful that my work is received by a wider readership, and is not merely a private venture.

Examples of Hindu–Christian studies today

Since I do not wish to over-identify the field of Hindu–Christian studies with my own work, it is fortunate that many works by other scholars can be noted, works that are scholarly and yet open to the nuances and complexities arising when one thinks across the Hindu–Christian border in a theologically sensitive way. Here I can name just a few – and my apologies in advance to the many other authors who might have been named here. None of the following works promotes itself as *the* model for the future of Hindu–Christian studies, and none of them dwells extensively on the concept of Hinduism itself; some do not characterize themselves as comparative theology, either. In choosing these figures, all holders of doctoral degrees, I stress the importance of professional training. But I do not think that the field need exclude learned individuals who have had neither the opportunity nor the preference for such studies. I introduce in turn recent works by Martin Ganeri, Ankur Barua, Jonathan Edelmann, Michelle Voss Roberts, and Chakravarthi Ram-Prasad.

Martin Ganeri's *Indian Thought and Western Theism: The Vedanta of Ramanuja* (2015) is very helpful in making explicit what is at stake and of value once we notice a commonality of certain forms of Hindu and Christian thought, and explore that commonality with adequate and non-reductive conceptual tools. He first of all provides us with an excellent overview of Thomism in relation to Vedanta in the 20th-century Indian context. While much attention has been paid to Sankara, Ramanuja too had played a role in Christian theology. Although attentive to the Jesuit project as a whole, Ganeri is particularly interested in how its scholastic bent was distinctively appropriate to engaging Vedanta. Ganeri reaffirms the "affinity between the Western scholastic tradition and that of scholastic Indian thought."[13] It creates the context in which the intellectual work of the Thomistic and Vedanta scholasticisms can be read and thought through together, differences noted and even argued more productively. He further observes that the "category of 'scholasticism' would seem to work as the best way of characterizing both Western and classical Indian thought." Indeed, "Ramanuja has much less in common with modern philosophy of religion in general and with modern Western forms of theism that manifest many of its distinctive features, and more in common with Aquinas than has previously been affirmed."[14] As for terminology, Ganeri thinks that "scholastic theology" is "certainly better than 'philosophy' and preferable even to a simple 'theology,' though 'theology' is itself better than 'philosophy.'"[15] The scholastic complexities of Vedanta and Thomism "arise because of the fact that they aim to keep hold of what their authoritative texts and traditions teach when combined with rigorous rational discussion. This fact, as well as the concepts of ultimate reality and of the world themselves, which are expressed through these complex discourses, mark out their approaches as other than modern philosophy of religion and modern forms of theism,"[16] and more capable of opening up ways of thinking about non-dualism, embodiment, and a conception of the God–world relationship that would (once again) be intellectually productive. It is lamentable, Ganeri says, that modern scholars of both the Christian and Hindu traditions have put aside scholastic tools even in the engagement of Western and Indian scholasticisms, since "a further use of Western scholastic concepts would at the very least help avoid the kind of misunderstanding that the use of concepts drawn from modern philosophy of religion or forms of Western theism can cause."[17] By the creative engagement of both Christian and Hindu scholastic modes of analysis and construction together, Ganeri thus opens up a viable version of Hindu–Christian studies that is open to those willing to work within the world of scholastic discourse rather than being entirely constrained by the expectations and rules of the modern academic study of religion.

Ankur Barua's *Debating "Conversion" in Hinduism and Christianity* (2015) takes up an issue that has been of concern throughout these lectures: whether fundamental faith claims and their intellectual and social implications render nearly impossible a proper space for a Hindu–Christian studies that is open, respectful, and capable of intellectual progress. Admitting that his book, though rich in historical detail, is not "a fine-grained historical survey of conversion movements,"[18] Barua elevates the discussion to a higher level of philosophical reflection by attending to the phenomenon of "epistemic peer conflict":

> Given that knowledgeable, sincere, and truth-seeking individuals across religious boundaries disagree over how to conceptualize the human predicament and the ultimate reality, is it possible to demonstrate that *one* of these is more consistent, coherent, and adequate than others on cognitive, experiential, and spiritual grounds?[19]

Hindu and Christian views of religion and religions, and the very idea of "Religion," need to be traced back to Christian and Hindu views of a particular sort and settled in particular locations. Barua brings expert epistemological insight to bear on the problem(s) of India and the West, and thus sheds light on key moments in the history of Hindu–Christian encounters. Conjoining good philosophical instincts with his solid knowledge of Christian theology, he revisits missionary encounters and also examines "mission" in terms of Hindu as well as Christian practice, Hindu and Christian rhetorics for and against conversions, and the contemporary situation of both Hindus and Christians in an Indian context that is more secular and yet also more subject to politicized religiosity today. Barua examines each issue fairly, and does not overlook even more strident critiques of the very idea of a Hindu–Christian rapprochement that is more than political posturing. He listens to the theological concerns that believers bring to debates over conversion and related matters. In this complex situation, it is to his credit that large questions remain open and difficult even at the volume's end, such as this question so very pertinent to Hindu–Christian studies:

> When Christian theological themes are woven into the fabric of Hindu cultural patterns, the process of transcreation leading to the emergence of distinctive forms of Indian Christianity, is the product an instance of an "irreparable damage" to both or a "fruitful synthesis" of both?[20]

Barua warns against expecting single answers to such questions. Even a successful response is unlikely to win unanimous support in one's own tradition, much less in another. It should not be a surprise that this is so; much of what I have sketched in the previous chapters of this book highlights the impossibility of any final resolution of problems relating to Hindu–Christian studies. But the work of comparative learning is still productive, even in its ever imperfect and provisional form.

Jonathan Edelmann's *Hindu Theology and Biology: The Bhagavata Purana and Contemporary Theory* (2012) is a constructive work seeking to draw evolutionary theory into dialogue with the Hindu tradition. The book is not primarily about Hindu–Christian studies nor a demonstration of the discipline's methodology (though it contributes to both), but about contemporary developments in evolutionary sciences that merit the attention of religious intellectuals across traditions. The book has a wide reach, and takes on a daring task and poses a double-edged challenge, since Edelmann asks scientists to take traditional Hindu learning seriously, just as he asks Hindu intellectuals to engage seriously the history of science, for example the biological, so as "to lift Hinduism out of history and into the cosmopolis of contemporary academia."[21] Distancing himself from easy and facile correspondences, such as "the Vedic view of biology" or the "Vedic anticipation of Darwinism," Edelmann seeks to draw the scientific community into conversation with the Hindu tradition. Conversely, he calls on scientists to be open to alternative, non-Western epistemologies and metaphysical bases for structuring our knowledge of and construction of reality; the challenge is to learn from Indian ways of analyzing reality and of debating any topic in science that opens into philosophical considerations. In particular, he asks them to pay attention to the Bhagavata Purana, a classic of Vaisnava theology and spirituality, as shedding light on the non-reductive interrelationships of body, mind, and consciousness in a way that may disentangle some of the problems that have vexed the Christian community.[22] His project is to make accessible and relevant the rational and empirical dimensions of Hindu constructions of reality, constructions which serve not to replace but rather only to ground freshly and from a new perspective scientific efforts to explain human being and human consciousness. This input from outside the Christian West will of course subject to review many of the old "science vs. religion" animosities in the West, and thereby contribute to the well-being of rational discourse on religious matters even beyond the Hindu–Christian context.

Michelle Voss Roberts' *Tastes of the Divine* (2014), written from a Christian perspective, demonstrates the possibility and value of taking as paradigmatic a systematic construction of reality evident in another tradition – namely, the Christian effort to take seriously and learn from the conceptualization of *rasa* proposed by Abhinavagupta. Voss Roberts draws on the heuristic categories of a non-Christian and non-Western tradition, eschewing all brief or casual references to Hinduism, etc. At the center of the book is the *rasa* schema that most likely originated in the *bharatanatyam* dance traditions and was later theorized by the great Kashmir Śaiva literary scholar, philosopher, and theologian Abhinavagupta (10th century). Voss Roberts draws on this material in order to bring experience, the aesthetic, and the emotions firmly into the center of her study. At other points in the book she draws also on some Western religious intellectuals of fame, such as Bernard of Clairvaux, when exploring embodied love, and Paul Tillich and Hans Urs von Balthasar, when expounding the Christian aesthetic vision of the world. After establishing theological foundations, she then moves to thinking through, from a Christian perspective informed by Dalit concerns, how the peaceful (*santa) rasa* can focus and heighten our attention to suffering. That she wishes to move from detachment – signified by the peaceful *rasa* – to three ways of engaging the world – love (in embodied, gendered experience), fury (in outrage at injustice), and wonder (in an openness that both resists doctrinal closure and inspires interreligious learning) – makes good sense in terms of the overall balancing act that is *Tastes of the Divine.* Still more might be said about the challenging difference that would remain if the peaceful *rasa* were afforded its traditional place as the final *rasa. Tastes of the*

Divine is a solid contribution to the discipline of comparative studies in an age of skepticism about the very idea of comparison. Already in the book's preface, Voss Roberts asks why and how a comparative study can be credibly undertaken even when it is narrowly posed, according to the preferences of the comparativist. As we know too well, comparison can be often judgmental, unfair to the Other, and predictably confirmatory of starting points. Responding by way of the example of her own work, she demonstrates how comparison, rather than merely privileging similarities for the sake of neater theories about the world or the human or the sacred, can succeed as a complex and multi-leveled academic project. As a whole, the book successfully helps us beyond several impasses that vex the study of Indian thought in the Western academy: the default tendency to make Hinduism merely the object of study but never the creator of the categories in which the study proceeds; the well-meant effort to protect Hinduism against bad comparisons by rejecting comparison altogether; and the heavy-handedness of a study of religion mode that rules out theological concerns and sensitivities for the sake of an elusive (if not evasive) neutrality. Even admitted biases, if honestly noted, can serve as resources for sound critical judgments.

Chakravarthi Ram-Prasad takes a comparative turn within the Hindu tradition itself in his *Divine Self, Human Self: The Philosophy of Being in Two Gita Commentaries* (2013), a substantive work of theology within his own tradition. It is by his account not a work of Indology or descriptive philosophical or theological study, nor even a primarily comparative study; rather, in the tradition of Matilal and Murty, I would say, it is a constructive contribution that draws on an ongoing conversation and debate between two Hindu traditions that have a long history and are alive today. Its comparative dimension is sharpened by the conviction that comparative learning is notably fruitful with respect to new insights into familiar issues. Though not posing as a theologian, he confesses that the book offers the fruits of long reflection by "someone from Ramanuja's Sri Vaisnava community who has worked on Sankara for half a lifetime."[23] By taking comparative work seriously, he seeks to contribute to constructive Hindu theology, a discipline too often denied and even deemed non-existent.[24] While Ram-Prasad does not discuss comparative theology and its methods in detail, he sees his work as exemplifying the method because he expounds and analyzes deep issues arising in the two commentaries which serve as the site for the deepest considerations of what it means to be human in the world and in God: "Unless one rejects outright the possibility of learning from another tradition, one will find discussions originally articulated in Christian theology illuminated and perhaps even re-shaped by the spiritual force of their ideas."[25] Ram-Prasad's implication, not developed in his book though envisioned in its introduction, is that theological exchange of this sort can create the basis for a fairer and more sophisticated encounter between Christian and Hindu thinkers.

I have mentioned just five out of numerous contemporary authors whose works might be recognized as instances of Hindu–Christian studies, even when they also contribute to other fields, such as historical study, poetics, science and religion, philosophy and comparative philosophy. Despite their diverse topics, these books share important intellectual and spiritual presuppositions and hopes that make possible empathetic constructions of the Other. They all value learning from more than one tradition, even as they recognize that this learning may render the "home" tradition vulnerable to revision in light of input from other traditions that hitherto were merely objects of study. As the field of Hindu–Christian studies is renewed on the ground, in practice, much more theological reflection across the Hindu–Christian border will be possible and required, undertaken by scholars mindful of their own tradition and the tradition of the other, each taken seriously in its potential and its limits. This work has happened; and therefore it *can* happen in the decades to come.

Within the shared space of Hindu–Christian studies

I conclude with several brief reflections. Within the limits of just three lectures leading to a small book, I have sought to make the case that a vital Hindu–Christian studies is a fundamentally theological project irreducible to historical investigations and ethnographic writing, or to the immediate possibilities and obligations of dialogue. Particularly in my first two lectures, I have hoped to traverse (in an only partly original way) some of the historical ground required if we are to note possibilities and ponder when and where potentially rich interreligious learning fell short. The field is still not free of its roots in Christian missionary tradition, and in the Indian philosophical engagement with Europe, and ought not to try to conceal or deny its past. It has needed constantly to purify itself of the blindnesses of that past, by academic study and by a responsible assessment of social issues. It has also had to resist the temptation to replace theology with pre- or anti-theological modes of inquiry, and to insist on expertise in depth and for the long term, beyond the often more passing events that often make up the history of interreligious dialogue.

At the start of this book, I mentioned the need to clear and enter into an intellectual and spiritual site – an intellectual and spiritual third space – where thoughtful practitioners of the two traditions could meet and learn mutually, authentic to their own traditions but benefitting from the other, all for the sake of a learning that neither tradition could attain on its own. While the term "third space" is merely useful and need not be thought to have arcane significance, it is important to recognize the need for a space other than the one of traditional Hindu–Christian encounters in India, where miscommunication was too often the norm, as one tradition tried to overcome the other or, conversely, to ignore the other completely. We need a space irreducible to what one community or the other thinks appropriate, but wherein learning fosters habitual reciprocity. Such a space will always be uneven and subject to tremors, but thus too free enough that in it the religious intellectuals of both traditions will learn what they would not have known otherwise, neither alien nor reducible to truths familiar to the traditions involved. From de Nobili on, reformers committed to interreligious learning have seen the importance of such spaces, often recognized as ashrams (even if they need not be ashrams). Others as well have testified to the importance of embodying the intellectual exchange in hospitable communal settings. Very admirably too, Hindu intellectuals have persisted in studying and thinking through the Christian West, even under very difficult circumstances when the fair and nurturing third space was largely missing. More specifically, it needs to be a space that has academic contours, as well as personal and more intimate practical versions.

By my reckoning, then, the best Hindu–Christian studies have within them, either explicitly or just beneath the surface, a working recognition of the importance of a faith grounded in one or another Hindu or Christian community, a connectedness to certain distinct yet harmonious forms of practice and theory, and movements of inquiry and appropriation grounded in the honest dynamics of two communities of believers encountering one another. To assert that the future of Hindu–Christian studies requires the form of theology, faith seeking understanding, faith lived out in intelligent practice, need not exclude a priori the writings of younger "spiritual but not religious" scholars, nor does it exclude those negotiating in a lower key the strictures of academic success; but it does propose a certain skepticism toward unanchored study, study which is merely distanced from faith and community and therefore gives no clues as to spiritual genealogy. It remains to be seen how seriously and deeply Hindus and Christians are ready to collaborate in the urgently needed Hindu–Christian conversation. For this to happen, venues such as the Westcott–Teape Lectures are all the more necessary, as new generations of scholars, in India and globally, think through the relations of our two traditions considered together. There is much work to be done, and we need to be able to recognize one another as kindred spirits, together in this work, for the betterment of ourselves and our world.

Notes

1 On my study of Hinduism as part of a project in comparative theology, see chapters 4 and 5 of my *Comparative Theology* (2010).
2 Cornille 2008: 4.
3 Ibid.
4 Ibid., 5.
5 Ibid.
6 Ibid., 6.
7 Sankara 1921: nn. 15–16
8 Ibid., n. 17
9 Ibid., nn. 18–21.
10 Ibid.., nn. 22–27.
11 Clooney 2005b: 234.
12 Clooney 2013: 140.
13 Ganeri 2015: 164.
14 Ibid.
15 Ibid.
16 Ibid.
17 Ibid.
18 Barua 2015: 1.
19 Ibid.
20 Ibid., 208.
21 Edelmann 2012: 216.
22 The main chapters of the book cover a wide range of topics, each taken up with attention to the Bhagavatam: "Ontology of Body, Mind, and Consciousness" (2), "Toward a Bhagavata Theory of Knowledge" (3), "The Study of Nature as Vaishnava Yoga" (4), "Seeing Truth, Hearing Truth" (5), and "Moving from Nature to God" (6).
23 Ram-Prasad 2013: xii.
24 Ibid., ix.
25 Ibid., x.

Bibliography

Anand Amaladass, SJ. "Viewpoints: Hindu–Christian Dialogue Today," *Journal of Hindu–Christian Studies* 10 (1997): 41–43.

Anand Amaladass, SJ, and Gudrun Löwner. *Christian Themes in Indian Art from the Mogul Times Till Today.* Manohar Publishers and Distributors, 2012.

Urs App. *The Birth of Orientalism.* University of Pennsylvania Press, 2010.

Christopher Baker. *The Hybrid Church in the City: Third Space Thinking.* Ashgate, 2007.

Ankur Barua. *Debating "Conversion" in Hinduism and Christianity.* Routledge, 2015.

S. N. Balagangadhara. *"The Heathen in His Blindness...": Asia, the West, and the Dynamic of Religion.* Leiden: E.J. Brill, 1994.

Homi Bhabha. *Location of Culture.* Routledge, 1994.

Krishna Chandra Bhattacaryya. "Swaraj in Ideas" (1929), in *Indian Philosophy in English: From Renaissance to Independence*, edited by Nalini Bhushan and Jay Garfield. Oxford University Press, 2011: 103–111.

Kristin Bloomer. "Comparative Theology, Comparative Religion, and Hindu–Christian Studies: Ethnography as Method," *Journal of Hindu–Christian Studies* 21 (2008): 33–42.

Delwin Brown and Linell Cady. *Religious Studies, Theology, and the University: Conflicting Maps, Changing Terrain.* State University of New York Press, 2002.

Jose Cabezón."The Discipline and Its Other: The Dialectic of Alterity in the Study of Religion," *Journal of the American Academy of Religion.* Thematic section, "On the Future of the Study of Religion in the Academy" 74.1 (2006a): 21–38.

Jose Cabezón. "In Defense of Abstraction: A Reply to William Schweiker," *Journal of the American Academy of Religion.* Thematic section, "On the Future of the Study of Religion in the Academy" 74.1 (2006b): 45–46.

Amita Chatterjee. "Brajendra Nath Seal: A Disenchanted Hegelian." In *Philosophy in Colonial India* (Sophia Studies in Cross-cultural Philosophy of Traditions and Cultures 11), edited by Sharad Deshpande. Springer, 2015: 81–101.

Margaret Chatterjee."The Prospect for Hindu–Christian Interaction." *Journal of Hindu–Christian Studies* 2 (1989): 2.

Francis X. Clooney, SJ. "Srivaisnavism in Dialogue, c. 1900: Alkondavilli Govindacharya as a Comparative Theologian," *Journal of Vaisnava Studies* 13. 1 (2004): 103–124.

Francis X. Clooney, SJ. *Fr. Bouchet's India: An 18th-Century Jesuit's Encounter with Hinduism*. Satya Nilayam Publications, 2005a.

Francis X. Clooney, SJ. *Divine Mother, Blessed Mother: Hindu Goddesses and the Virgin Mary*. Oxford University Press, 2005b.

Francis X. Clooney, SJ. *Comparative Theology: Deep Learning across Religious Borders*. Wiley-Blackwell, 2010.

Francis X. Clooney, SJ. *His Hiding Place Is Darkness: Toward a Hindu–Catholic Theopoetics of Divine Absence*. Stanford University Press, 2013.

Francis X. Clooney, SJ. "Hindu–Christian Traditions Together: Theological Reasons for Mutual Respect and Reverence," in *Commemorative Brochure: Hindu–Christian Dialogue*. United States Conference of Catholic Bishops, May 23, 2015 .

Fred Clothey, "Hindu-Christian 'Studies': Some Confessions from the Boundaries," *Hindu–Christian Studies Bulletin* 9 (1996): 42–45.

Gaston-Laurent Coeurdoux, SJ. *Moeurs et Coutumes des Indiens* (1777), in Sylvia Murr. *L'Inde Philosophique entre Bousset et Voltaire*, Vol. 2. École française d'Extrême Orient, 1987.

Catherine Cornille. *The (Im)possibility of Interreligious Dialogue*. The Crossroad Publishing Company, 2008.

Harold Coward. "A Retrospective of Hindu–Christian Studies: Establishment of the Journal and Formation of the Society," *Journal of Hindu–Christian Studies* 21 (2008): 3–10.

Jenny Daggers. "Thinking 'Religion': The Christian Past and Interreligious Future of Religious Studies and Theology," *Journal of the American Academy of Religion* 78.4 (2010): 961–990.

Roberto de Nobili, SJ. *Apology (c.* 1610). Typescript. Jesuit Archives, Chembaghanur, India. Translated by Augustin Saulière, SJ.

Roberto de Nobili, SJ. *Dispelling of Ignorance (*c. 1640). Typescript. Jesuit Archives, Chembaghanur, India. Translated by Augustin Saulière, SJ.

Roberto de Nobili, SJ. *Inquiry into the Meaning of "God" (c.* 1610). Translated in *Preaching Wisdom to the Wise: Three Treatises by Roberto de Nobili*. Edited by Anand Amaladass, SJ, and Francis X. Clooney, SJ. Institute of Jesuit Sources, 2000a: 305–323.

Roberto de Nobili, SJ. *Report on Indian Customs (*1615c.). Translated in *Preaching Wisdom to the Wise: Three Treatises by Roberto de Nobili*. Edited by Anand Amaladass, SJ, and Francis X. Clooney, SJ. St. Louis: Institute of Jesuit Sources, 2000b: 53–231.

Richard de Smet. "Sankara Vedanta and Christian Theology," in *Understanding Sankara: Essays by Richard de Smet*. Edited by Ivo Coelho. Motilal Banarsidass, 2013a: 383–397.

Richard de Smet. "Upadhyay's Interpretation of Sankara," in *Understanding Sankara: Essays by Richard de Smet*. Edited by Ivo Coelho. Motilal Banarsidass, 2013b: 454–462.

Mariasusai Dhavamony, SJ. *Love of God according to Saiva Siddhanta*. Oxford University Press, 1971.

Mariasusai Dhavamony, SJ. *Teachers of Religions: Christianity and Other Religions*. Gregorian University, 1988.

Mariasusai Dhavamony, SJ. "Evangelization and Dialogue," in *Vatican II: Assessment and Perspectives Twenty-five Years After (1962–1987)*, edited by René Latourelle. Paulist Press, 1989: 264–281.

Sean Doyle. *Synthesizing the Vedanta: The Theology of Pierre Johanns, SJ*. Peter Lang, 2006.

Francis X. D'Sa, SJ. *Sabdapramanyam in Sabara and Kumarila: Towards a Study of the Minamasa Experience of Language*. Institut für Indologie der Universität Wien, 1980.

Francis X. D'Sa, SJ. *Gott der Dreieine und der All-Ganze: Vorwort zur Begegnung zwischen Christentum un Hinduismus*. Patmos, 1987.

Jonathan B. Edelmann. *Hindu Theology and Biology: The Bhagavata Purana and Contemporary Theory*. Oxford University Press, 2012.

Jonathan B. Edelmann. "Becoming Different: Why Education Is Required for Responding to Globalism Dharmically," *Journal of Hindu–Christian Studies* 26 (2013): 17–27.

Gavin Flood. "Reflections on Tradition and Inquiry in the Study of Religion," *Journal of the American Academy of Religion*. Thematic section, "On the Future of the Study of Religion in the Academy" 74.1 (2006): 47–58.

Gavin Flood. *The Truth Within: A History of Inwardness in Christianity, Hinduism, and Buddhism*. Oxford University Press, 2013.

Martin Ganeri, OP. *Indian Thought and Western Theism: The Vedanta of Ramanuja*. Routledge, 2015.

Algondavilli Govindacharya. *Three Lectures on Inspiration, Intuition, and Ecstasy*. Wesleyan Mission Press, 1897.

Algondavilli Govindacharya. *The Divine Wisdom of the Dravida Saints*. C. N. Press, 1902a.

Algondavilli Govindacharya. *The Holy Lives of the Alvars*. G. T. A. Press, 1902b.

Algondavilli Govindacharya. *Mazdaism in the Light of Vishnuism*. G. T. A. Press, 1913.

Algondavilli Govindacharya. *A Metapysique of Mysticism Vedically Viewed*. Vasanta Press, 1923.

Sara Grant, RSCJ. *Towards an Alternative Theology: Confessions of a Non-Dualist Christian*. Asian Trading Corporation, 1991.

Sara Grant, RSCJ, and Swami Amalraj. "Response to This Letter from the Ashram Aikiya Satsangis," in Vandana Mataji (ed.), *Christian Ashrams: A Movement with a Future?* ISPCK, 1993: 157–160.

Xavier Gravend-Tirole. "From Christian Ashrams to Dalit Theology – or Beyond," in *Constructing Indian Christianities: Culture, Conversion and*

Caste, edited by Chad M. Bauman and Richard Fox Young. Routledge, 2014: 101–137.

Wilhelm Halbfass. *India and Europe: An Essay in Understanding*. State University of New York Press, 1988.

Edward Hulmes. *The Spalding Trust and the Union for the Study of the Great Religions: H. N. Spalding's Pioneering Vision*. The Memorial Club, 2002.

Ronald Inden. *Imagining India*. Basil Blackwell, 1990.

William A. Jarvis. *William Marshall Teape and His Lectures*. South Hylton Parish Church, 1990.

Pierre Johanns, SJ. *To Christ through the Vedanta*. 2 volumes. Compiled by Theo de Greeff. United Theological College, 1996.

Klaus K. Klostermeier. "A Literary Hindu–Christian Dialogue A Century Ago: Still Actual?" *Journal of Hindu–Christian Studies* 24 (2011): 31–35.

Jeffrey Kripal. *Kali's Child*. University of Chicago Press, 1998.

Daya Krishna. "A Plea for a New History of Philosophy in India," in *New Perspectives in Indian Philosophy*. Rawat Publications, 2001: 1–9.

Daya Krishna. "Comparative Philosophy: What It Is and What It Ought to Be," in *Interpreting across Boundaries*, edited by Gerald J. Larson and Eliot Deutsch. Princeton University Press, 2014: 71–83.

Oliver Lacombe. "La pensée catholique traditionelle et l'hindouisme," *Le Monde non chrétien*, October–December 1951: 387–401.

Nancy Levene. "Response to Gavin Flood, 'Reflections on Tradition and Inquiry in the Study of Religion,'" *Journal of the American Academy of Religion*. Thematic section, "On the Future of the Study of Religion in the Academy." 74.1 (2006): 59–63.

Julius Lipner. *Brahmabandhab Upadhyay: The Life and Thought of a Revolutionary*. Oxford University Press, 1999.

Rajiv Malhotra. *Being Different: An Indian Challenge to Western Universalism*. HarperCollins, 2011.

Rajiv Malhotra. "Author's Response: Cognitive Science, History-Centrism and the Future of Hindu Studies," *Journal of Hindu–Christian Studies* 26 (2013): 28–47.

Rajiv Malhotra. *The Battle for Sanskrit: Is Sanskrit Political or Sacred? Oppressive or Liberating? Dead or Alive?* HarperCollins, 2016.

Bradley Malkovsky. "Editor's Introduction," *Journal of Hindu-Christian Studies* 26 (2013): 1.

Suzanne L. Marchand. *German Orientalism in the Age of Empire: Religion, Race, and Scholarship*. Cambridge University Press, 2009.

Bimal Krishna Matilal. "Indian Philosophy: Is There a Problem Today?" in *Philosophy, Culture and Religion: The Collected Essays of Bimal Krishna Matilal, Vol. 1: Mind, Language and World*. Edited by Jonardon Ganeri. Oxford University Press, 2002a: 351–357.

Bimal Krishna Matilal. "The Logical Illumination of Indian Mysticism," in *Philosophy, Culture and Religion: The Collected Essays of Bimal Krishna Matilal, Vol. 1: Mind, Language and World*. Edited by Jonardon Ganeri. Oxford University Press, 2002b: 38–64.

Bimal Krishna Matilal. "The Problem of Inter-faith Studies," in *Philosophy, Culture and Religion: The Collected Essays of Bimal Krishna Matilal, Vol. 2: Ethics and Epics.* Oxford University Press, 2002c: 161–165.

Sylvia Murr. *L'Inde Philosophique entre Bousset et Voltaire.* 2 vols. École française d'Extrême Orient, 1987.

K. Satchidananda Murty. *The Realm of Between: Lectures on the Philosophy of Religion.* Indian Institute of Advanced Study, 1973.

K. Satchidananda Murty. *Revelation and Reason in Advaita Vedanta.* Motilal Banarsidass, 1959.

Andrea Nehring and Perry Schmidt-Leukel, eds. *Interreligious Comparisons in Religious Studies and Theology: Comparison Revisited.* Bloomsbury, 2016.

Hugh Nicholson. *Comparative Theology and the Problem of Religious Rivalry.* Oxford University Press, 2011.

Dan O'Connor. *Relations in Religion.* Allied Publishers, 1994.

Rudolph Otto. *Mysticism East and West.* Translated by Bertha L. Bracey and Richenda C. Payne. The Macmillan Company, 1932.

Parimal Patil."A Hindu Theologian's Response: A Prolegomenon to 'Christian God, Hindu God' (Afterword)," in *Hindu God, Christian God: How Reason Breaks Down the Boundaries between Religions,* by Francis X. Clooney, SJ. Oxford University Press, 2001: 185–195.

Ignatius Puthiadam, SJ. *God in the Thought of St. Thomas Aquinas and Sri Madhvacarya.* Sri L.D. Swamikannu Pillai Endowment Lectures 1978–1979, University of Madras.

Ignatius Puthiadam, SJ. *Visnu, the Ever Free: A Study of the Madhva Concept of God.* Dialogue Series, 1985.

Sarvepalli Radhakrishnan. *The World's Unborn Soul.* Clarendon Press, 1936.

Sarvepalli Radhakrishnan. "Meeting of Religions," in *Eastern Religions and Western Thought.* Oxford University Press, 1939: 306–348.

S. Rajamanickam. *The First Oriental Scholar.* De Nobili Research Institute, 1972.

Anantanand Rambachan. *The Advaita Worldview: God, World, and Humanity.* State University of New York Press, 2006.

Anantanand Rambachan. "The Traditional Roots of Difference," *Journal of Hindu–Christian Studies* 26 (2013): 2–9.

Anantanand Rambachan. *A Hindu Theology of Liberation.* State University of New York Press, 2015.

Chakravarthi Ram-Prasad. *Divine Self, Human Self: The Philosophy of Being in Two Gita Commentaries.* Bloomsbury, 2013.

Chakravarthi Ram-Prasad. "Reading the *Acaryas*: A Generous Conception of the Theological Method," *Journal of Hindu Studies* 7 (2014): 98–112.

Charles E. Raven. *Hinduism and Christianity: A Neglected Crisis.* Spottiswoode, Ballantyne and Company, Ltd., 1955. Bob Robinson. *Christians Meeting Hindus: An Analysis and Theological Critique of the Hindu–Christian Encounter in India.* Regnum, 2004.

T. S. Rukmani. "Dr. Richard de Smet and Sankara's Advaita," *Journal of Hindu–Christian Studies* 16 (2003): 12–21.

T. S. Rukmani. "Methodological Approaches to Hindu-Christian Studies: Some Thoughts," *Journal of Hindu–Christian Studies* 21 (2008): 43–47.

Tinu Ruparell. "Hindu Occidentalism," *Journal of Hindu–Christian Studies* 13 (2000): 26–31.

Sankara. *The Crest Jewel of Discrimination.* Translated by Swami Madhavananda. Advaita Ashrama, 1921.

Jan Peter Schouten. *Jesus as Guru: The Image of Christ among Hindus and Christians in India.* Rodopi, 2008.

Robert Schreiter. *The New Catholicity: Theology between the Global and the Local.* Orbis, 1997.

Raymond Schwab. *The Oriental Renaissance: Europe's Rediscovery of India and the East, 1680–1880.* Translated by Gene Patterson-Black and Victor Reinking. Columbia University Press, 1984.

William Schweiker. "The Discipline(s) and Its (Their) Other(s): A Response to José Ignacio Cabezón," *Journal of the American Academy of Religion.* Thematic section, "On the Future of the Study of Religion in the Academy." 74.1 (2006): 39–44.

Brajendranath Seal. *Comparative Studies in Vaishnavism and Christianity with an Examination of the Mahabharata Legend about Narada's Pilgrimage to Svetadvipa and an Introduction to the Historico-Comparative Method.* Hare Press, 1899.

Arvind Sharma. *Religious Studies and Comparative Methodology: The Case for Reciprocal Illumination.* State University of New York Press, 2005.

Noel Sheth, SJ. "Hindu Avatara and Christian Incarnation: A Comparison," *Philosophy East and West* 52.1 (2002): 98–125.

Jonathan Z. Smith. *Relating Religion: Essays in the Study of Religion.* University of Chicago Press, 2004.

George Soares-Prabhu, SJ. "From Alienation to Inculturation: Some Reflections on Doing Theology in India Today," in *Bread and Breath: Essays in Honor of Samuel Rayan, SJ.*, edited by T. K. John. Gujarat Sahitya Prakash, 1991: 55–99.

George Soares-Prabhu, SJ. "Letter from Fr. G. Soares-Prabhu to Vandana Mataji," in *Christian Ashrams: A Movement with A Future?, edited* by Vandana Mataji. ISPCK, 1993: 153–156.

Edward W. Soja. *Thirdspace: Journeys to Los Angeles and Other Real-and-Imagined Places.* Blackwell, 1996.

William Marshall Teape. *The Secret Lore of India and the One Perfect Life for All, Being a Few Main Passages from the Upanisads.* W. Heffer, 1932.

Swami Tyagananda and Pravrajika Vrajaprana. *Interpreting Ramakrishna.* Motilal Banarsidass Publishers, 2010.

Brahmabandhab Upadhay. *The Writings of Brahmabandhab Upadhay*, Vol. II. Abridged and annotated by Julius Lipner and George Gispert-Sauch. The United Theological College, 2002.

John Vattanky. *Ganesa's Philosophy of God: Analysis, Text, Translation, and Interpretation of Isvaravada Section of Gangesa's Tattvacintamani with a*

Study of the Development of Nyaya Theism. Adyar Library and Research Centre, 1984.

Michelle Voss Roberts. *Tastes of the Divine*. Fordham University Press, 2014.

William Wallace, SJ. "An Introduction to the Hindoo Philosophy." Unpublished manuscript. 1909. Archived at the Goethals Library, St. Xavier's, Kolkata.

William Wallace, SJ. *From Evangelical to Catholic by Way of the East*. Catholic Orphan Press, 1923.

Brooke Foss Westcott. *On Some Points in Religious Office of the Universities*. Macmillan, 1873.

Ulrich Winkler, "Reasons for and Contexts of Deep Theological Engagement with Other Religious Traditions in Europe: Toward a Comparative Theology," in *Comparative Theology in Europe*, edited by Francis X. Clooney , SJ, and John H. Berthrong. MDPI Publishing, 2014: 5–20.

Angela Barreto Xavier and Ines G. Županov. *Catholic Orientalism: Portuguese Empire, Indian Knowledge (16th–18th Centuries)*. Oxford University Press, 2015.

Robert C. Zaehner. *Foolishness to the Greeks*. Clarendon Press, 1953.

Ines G. Županov. *Disputed Mission: Jesuit Experiments and Brahmanical Knowledge in Seventeenth-Century India*. Oxford University Press, 1999.

Index

For Product Safety Concerns and Information please contact our EU representative GPSR@taylorandfrancis.com
Taylor & Francis Verlag GmbH, Kaufingerstraße 24, 80331 München, Germany

www.ingramcontent.com/pod-product-compliance
Ingram Content Group UK Ltd.
Pitfield, Milton Keynes, MK11 3LW, UK
UKHW021424080625
459435UK00011B/143